DISCARD

DEMCO

YOU
AIN'T GOT
NO EASTER
CLOTHES

YOU
AIN'T GOT
NO EASTER
CLOTHES

&

Laura Love

HYPERION

NEW YORK

Library of Congress Cataloging-in-Publication Data

Love, Laura.
    You ain't got no Easter clothes / Laura Love.
      p. cm.
    ISBN 1-4013-0011-1
    1. Love, Laura.   2. African American singers—Biography.
  I. Title.

ML420.L8853A3 2004
782.42164'092—dc22
[B]

2004047327

Hyperion books are available for special promotions and premiums. For details contact Michael Rentas, Manager, Inventory and Premium Sales, Hyperion, 77 West 66th Street, 11th floor, New York, New York 10023, or call 212-456-0133.

FIRST EDITION

10 9 8 7 6 5 4 3 2 1

For Pam, Mary, Lisa, and Gigantor

PROLOGUE

Sometime in the year 2000 I began writing everything down. I wanted to write as if no one else would ever read these words—without concern for how I would be judged as I related my worst deeds and greatest epiphanies. My earliest memories are of hard times living in Nebraska in the 1960s, and the desperate measures my mother took to cope with mental illness and single motherhood. They are memories of foster homes, orphanages, upheaval, racism, and disaster tempered by outrageous bits of fortune and love. The events that I have written about in this book describe what it was like for my sister, Lisa, and me to grow up in the midst of my mother's chaos. Time after time we were thrust into calamity and somehow found humor and hope in the strangest places.

In 1982 my mother disappeared from the apartment where she'd lived for the last five years, and I was unable to find her. I was twenty-two, living in Portland, Oregon, at the time, and had not been able to reach her by phone or mail for months. I called her neighbor and asked him if he knew anything of her whereabouts. He told me there had been a suspicious fire in her apartment and that she had been rescued by a hook and ladder team that had assisted her from her second-story window to the safety of the parking lot. He said he had not seen her since that day.

For the next sixteen years I continued to search for her. As a recording artist for Mercury Records, I was able to enlist help in finding her from those who read my CD liner notes. So many kind and generous people wrote to me and lent themselves to the effort, and I was touched by their caring. Often, between the songs I performed in concert, I described life in Nebraska in the 1960s, from my perspective as a light-skinned black girl, trying to survive childhood with my paranoid-schizophrenic mother. As I look back at our lives, situations that once seemed impossible to live through can sometimes now send me into fits of laughter, as I recall their absurdity. Carol Burnett once said, "Comedy is tragedy plus time." My family proved her right again and again.

Some of these stories may be difficult to read, and I wrestled with thoughts of omitting them, but in the end, I decided to tell them as faithfully as possible to try and repay people who have helped me all along the way. I was often asked by my listeners to compile the family stories that I had spoken of onstage and written about in my liner notes. This memoir is an attempt to honor those requests.

YOU
AIN'T GOT
NO EASTER
CLOTHES

WINI

She sat on the toilet throwing up between her legs as she buttoned my dress. I had my back to her and I remember being afraid to turn around. I knew that something big was happening. My mother was crying and so was I. I'm not sure where my sister was. A single bulb hung over our heads, barely illuminating the bathroom. The next thing I remember we were sitting in the back of a police car. It was the middle of the night. A white police officer was driving and my mother sat alongside him. She was looking through the window with her head pressed to the glass, seemingly unaware that Lisa and I were right there behind her. The car stopped and the officer opened the door and let us out at the bottom of a flight of cement stairs. Those stairs seemed to go all the way to the sky. We reached the top of the stairs and someone opened the door and told us to hurry up and get inside. My mother didn't say good-bye. She didn't seem to know we were going anywhere— that we would be separated. That's how we got to Cedar's Home for Children.

I was three years old that winter. It was 1963, and we were in Lincoln, Nebraska. I still feel completely alone when I think of it almost forty years later. That first night Lisa and I were put in the same bed by a woman named Lottie, and I could hear other kids all around us, breathing, moaning, sighing, coughing. I woke up cold and wet and looked at myself under the covers. My sister had peed the bed.

Lottie, the woman in charge, hated kids: "Don't puke till I get the bucket, goddammit, don't you puke yet." ... "She ain't your sister." ... "She's colored and you ain't." ... "Can't nobody even get a brush through that wool." I remember snot ... cold ... cement. I remember being hungry, always hungry. I remember Spam, white bread, and butter, and that there was never enough. I remember a chain-link fence and mean-ass white boys, big enough to hurt you. They told me to sit in the front of the wagon, that they'd push me. They pushed all right. They pushed that thing right into a yellow-painted cinder-block wall and I felt my head explode. I bled and bled and bled. Lottie walked over, mad. She snatched me by the arm and dragged me up to the room where creaky iron cots were lined up. I was put in bed. I knew that I was hated. She told me not to bleed on the pillow or "I'll paddle your ass." I didn't think that the Band-Aid would hold the blood back, but I hoped anyway. I woke up in the middle of the night and put my pillow up to the window to see it in the light that shone through from outside. There was blood on it. I turned it over to make the blood disappear and tried to fall asleep. When I think of Lottie I think of soap and what it tasted like. My mother might have been crazy, but she sure as hell wasn't stupid. My mother knew how to talk. Lottie was trash. My mother would have hated Lottie. I hated Lottie and so did my sister, Lisa.

Almost a year later, when I was nearly four, Lisa and I got to pick out shoes donated by a local charity. I wanted the saddle shoes, but they didn't fit, so instead I got shoes with a buckle that I liked almost as much. Lisa got new shoes, too. We were going to visit my mother for the first time in a long time, and it seemed the staff at Cedar's thought we looked too shabby to be going out in public. People kept saying, "You wanna look nice to see your mama, don't you?" I did, but I was also scared.

I didn't say a word to Lisa during the entire car ride to the hospital. I am still ashamed to admit that I avoided her that whole year at Cedar's because everything about her reminded me of that awful night, the night our mother changed and then disappeared. Lisa often cried and would say, "Hi, Lauri . . . C'mere, Lauri . . . Don't go, Lauri." But I did go. I was goddamned if I was going to be around anything that took me back to that day in that place with those people. If that meant cutting Lisa off with her wild nappy hair and huge eyes, so be it. Besides, Lottie said she wasn't my sister anyway. She said I was a white girl and that I couldn't have a colored sister.

And then, there she stood—Wini, my mommy. Or at least she looked like my mother, but her eyes were so dead. Every move she made seemed strenuous. She looked skinny and tired. Now I know that she had undergone massive shock treatments for the better part of that year at the Nebraska State Hospital and that much of her memory and affect had disappeared as a result. When she finally spoke, she asked if we were her sisters. She wanted to know if Lisa and I were there to play with her. That scared me. Pretty soon we left. I didn't care if we never went back there again.

A couple of weeks later, on Christmas Eve, Lisa and I were in a van with a bunch of other kids. I sat there crying and crying because they told us we were going home to be with our mommy. "Home" meant Cedar's now, and as awful as that was, I was used to it and I didn't want to go and be with the zombie. Lisa seemed happy to be leaving. And then, suddenly, we were at the front door of our house on Forty-ninth Street. My mother bent over, crying and kissing me and Lisa, and she seemed like a real mother. She brought us inside and we said good-bye to the kids we'd lived with for the better part of a year. Mommy kept on crying and saying how thin we were and how we were just going to eat and eat. We opened presents as she watched us. I thought it odd that she didn't seem to know what was in the packages before they were opened. I opened one with a Barbie doll inside. I was thrilled, but my mom had a look of disgust on her face. She kept saying, "That's not a baby doll." She never liked Barbies. She thought they were cheap and vulgar. I now think so, too, but seeing the prices they fetch at auctions makes me wish I still had that Barbie in that box with those clothes on it.

A couple of days later we got Ting, a Siamese cat. Jane and Dwight Morris brought her over. Dwight taught at Nebraska Wesleyan University, a block away, where my mom now attended college, compliments of a social services agency whose staff liked my mom, or probably just felt sorry for her. Jane baby-sat for us while Mom was at school.

Ting had blue eyes and a brown face, ears, and paws. God, we were mean to that cat. We loved Jane Morris though. Her cats were Scheherazade and Sredni Vashtar. We loved to say those names. One of her cats was always having kittens. We couldn't wait to go to Jane and

Dwight's house. It felt safe there. We also loved their two boys, Johnny and Tommy Morris. Jane hardly ever got mad at me and Lisa. Her house radiated normalcy and goodness. She made baloney sandwiches for lunch, and they ate lunch at the same time every day.

When Dwight came home at night he always brought my mom with him in his white Volkswagen, and she would put our coats on and we'd walk home. One time there was so much snow on the ground that it came to my waist where the sidewalk hadn't been shoveled. Mom led us, walking fast and not looking behind her. She seemed to wish Lisa and I would disappear. She was overloaded with school and work and we often felt we were in her way. My teeth chattered and I couldn't get over the look and feel of the snow. Some of it had fallen inside my boots. I called, "Mommy, wait ... please, my hands are cold and I can't keep up." She looked back with sheer hatred and said, "Shut up." Sometimes I would hide from her in a closet when she came to Jane's to pick us up. Jane would say, "Come out of there—your mommy will feel bad if you hide." I remember telling her I was just joking, but she said Mommy wouldn't know that and wouldn't like it. I came out but I didn't want to.

One time over at Jane's there were a whole bunch of kittens in a back bedroom. I wanted to see them, and when I walked in I was overcome by a feeling of tenderness and love for them. I picked them up one by one and rubbed my cheeks against them. I loved them so much, and I wanted them to understand this and to feel the same way about me. I petted them and held them close to my face and then, for some reason, I began to feel unhappy with them for not loving me back—for not showing me that they loved me. I wanted them to purr and look at me, and they wouldn't even open their eyes. That's when I started to throw them against the wall. One or two and finally all of them. They mewed and cried as I threw them up into the ceiling over and over. Then I walked out of the room calmly and told Jane, "Something's wrong with the kittens—they're bleeding." Jane walked into that bedroom while I stayed out in the living room and I'm not sure what happened after that. I do know that things got very quiet. I never got punished for it, but Jane and everyone around me talked to me differently and looked at me differently.

I am forty-one years old now and the two things in my life I wish I could undo are running from my sister at Cedar's and throwing those kittens around. I don't know if they lived or died, but I wake up sometimes now crying about those two things. Despite what I did to the kittens, Jane was always kind to me. Once she chastised me for misbehaving—she told me to go into her bedroom and sit there. About an hour later she came into the room and I was lying on the bed cooling off and being sad while the tears on my face dried. She reached over and pulled me into her lap and hugged me and held on to me and rocked me in this way that felt so warm and safe and good. I remember thinking, I wish she could do this to me every day of my life and knowing then that I thought I loved her more than my mommy, and thinking that that was wrong. We wished Jane could have been our baby-sitter forever, but some months later the Morrises moved to the town of Hastings, Nebraska, and adopted a little girl named Annie Sue, becoming the first white couple in our state to adopt a black child.

Mildred was our next baby-sitter. She was nuts. She was the oldest woman I had ever seen. Mildred smelled like some kind of bowel rot from deep inside her was seeping from her pores and out of her mouth. I don't know what kind of a deal my mom got on her, but whatever it was, it wasn't enough. When Mom went off to college every day, all day, she would leave us with Mildred, who would put us back in bed the minute Mom was gone. At some point in the afternoon she would let us get up and go out in the yard, where we were to pick up sticks all day. The only thing worse than picking up sticks was staying in bed half the day, bored out of our minds.

Once, she went into my mom's dresser drawer and cut up her underwear into pieces and told us to dust the house with them. We told her that the underwear weren't rags and we shouldn't be cutting them up and dusting with them. Mildred didn't want to hear this though, and when my mom came home from school she wasn't at all happy with her. Another time, when Mildred thought we were sleeping, we snuck out of our bedroom window and ran the whole block to Mom's campus. She happened to be outdoors with her class and we spotted her instantly. We knew we weren't allowed to cross the street, so we stood there and wailed from the other side, begging her to come home and make Mildred leave. I'm sure that we embarrassed her; the whole class stopped and gaped at us, crying and screaming for Mommy to come home and get rid of Mildred. I think that might have been the last time Mildred sat with us, because I don't remember seeing her after that. By then I was four and a half, and Lisa was nearly ready to start kindergarten. Things were especially tense then. We knew our job was to shut up and stay out of the way so Mom could study.

One morning Lisa and I got up while Mommy was still in bed. I was bored and we had not gotten our first black-and-white TV yet, so I turned on the electric stove for entertainment. Lisa's eyes got huge and she said, "No, Lauri, Mommy will get mad," and I told her to be quiet because Mommy was never going to know. Somehow or other I got pretty caught up in the turning on and off of knobs and started noticing that some burners were getting really red. I wanted to get those burners off bad, but I just couldn't seem to accomplish it. Lisa looked at me with this desperate kind of pleading in her eyes as we began to hear our mother stirring in the next room. Quick—think, think, think—how do I do this? And somehow, miraculously, they were all off, and the red coils started getting black again. Thank God. Just in the nick of time. I looked smugly at my sister and said, "I told you so," as we sat at the kitchen table and quietly waited for my mother to enter the room.

A few seconds later she came in. I was very slick, I was thinking—so smooth.

Then my mother said to me, "Lauri, were you girls playing with the stove?" Dammit, how in the hell did she know?

I looked her straight in the eye and said, "No, Mommy, we weren't." My heart was pounding but I thought I was doing reasonably well maintaining my cool, giving nothing away.

"Uh-huh, I see," said my mommy, nodding reassuringly, and even smiling a little. "You weren't playing with the stove—that's what you're telling me?" Oh boy, look at her—she's taking my word for it. I have finally learned to lie convincingly.

"No, Mommy, we weren't playing with the stove, because you told us not to."

"So what you're telling me then, is that you and Lisa *were not* just playing with the stove before I walked into the room?"

"No, Mommy, me and Lisa weren't just playing with the stove before you walked into the room."

"Well, that's good, Lauri, because if you *were* playing with the stove and the burner was still hot, I know you wouldn't let Mommy burn her hand by touching it, would you? Because Mommy believes you when you say you weren't playing with the stove before I walked into the room."

By then I was in so deep I had to go with it. "No," I said, weakly. "No, me and Lisa weren't playing with the stove," I repeated, shaking my head for emphasis.

She said quietly, "So I guess you wouldn't mind it then, if I did this." And with that she pushed her whole hand, palm down, onto the burner that had been red as a baboon's ass a few seconds ago, and let fly a blood-curdling scream that filled the air and probably the whole neighborhood with the sound of it. She seemed to hold her hand on that burner forever and I saw smoke curling up and smelled this awful stink that was like charred toenails or hair. But it was my mother's hand. She pulled it back, finally, and there was a seared coil imprint of that burner right there in the flesh of her hand. She looked at me with dead, dull eyes and said slowly and evenly, "Don't you ever play with the stove again—do you hear me?" I never did.

DOWN THE STAIRS

&

N ot *long after that we* moved from the house on Forty-ninth
Street to live in Mrs. Makosky's basement. We'd gotten behind
on our rent in the old place and been forced to vacate the premises. I
don't know how Mrs. Makosky could justify any amount of rent for the
new place, which was a damp, water bug–and-cockroach-infested space.

Mrs. Makosky ran an informal day care upstairs in her part of the
house for working mothers who could afford her services. My mother
was not among them. On the rare occasions when Mom did leave us
with Mrs. Makosky, I was always amazed at the difference in the way
the upstairs felt as compared to the basement, where we lived. Mrs.
Makosky, who was in her late sixties, had a house that looked like any

old lady's, with walls pleasantly papered and windows trimmed with cheery pastel yellow curtains. The comfortable furnishings matched and all of the floors were finished with carpet or linoleum. Her bed, in sharp contrast to the odds and ends we had become used to, had a headboard, frame, box spring, and mattress, and was covered with a complete set of matching sheets and a comforter. The radio was always tuned to Paul Harvey and there were kids' toys neatly stored about the house. She was the first person I ever noticed wearing false teeth.

She seemed nice enough with the white kids that she watched every day, but seemed uneasy around us. Once in a while, Mrs. Makosky reluctantly agreed to watch my sister and me while our mom was at college taking a test or studying late. She would invariably take us upstairs and drill us on matters of personal hygiene. Tooth brushing was a particular obsession of hers, and she would lecture us endlessly on the need to spend as much time brushing one's tongue as one's teeth. She insisted that the tongue carried as much, if not more, bacteria than the teeth, and that she who was wise enough to pay attention to this little-known fact would be rewarded with a healthy smile long into her dotage. While Mrs. Makosky was reasonably kind to us, every time she had a visitor while we were in her care, she would shepherd us into the back bedroom and warn us to stay put. Mom told us Mrs. Makosky was hiding us away because she thought it demeaning for a white woman to tend black children. She made the task less onerous by imagining herself a missionary among savages. When we went back downstairs from her bright kitchen it was like stepping into a parallel universe. The basement had concrete floors and a shower nozzle in one corner with an open drain and pipes and wires and floor joists exposed everywhere. Every night when we turned off the light, a single bare bulb, the place came alive. Black, shiny water bugs as big as a man's thumb swarmed the entire floor until it looked like the whole thing was moving. They crawled through the drains, up the walls, onto the beds, onto the curtains—everywhere. Lisa and I both slept on a fold-out couch in the "living room" and when I had to get up to pee, I would turn on a light and watch the bugs scatter from the folds of our bedding. I was scared to go to sleep, scared to wake up, scared to walk on the floor, scared to wake my mother up, just scared.

By 1965 I was bursting at the seams to start kindergarten. Though Mom was constantly overwhelmed, she always made time to read and sing to us, which instilled an early love for books and music. I had watched Lisa start her schooling the year before and had been filled with envy of her new adventures. My teacher, Miss George, was young and pretty and impressed that I knew all my numbers and ABCs and could even read a little bit before I got there. She used to put on some sort of drum-heavy record and have us all "dance like Indians" and say "woooo wooo wooooo" while we slapped the "O" holes our mouths made. I was proud when Miss George noticed my Indian dancing skills, though I tried to feign modesty. "Bobby Hertz does a good one, too," I said, trying to share the wealth. I said this even though I knew my Indian was better than his. It never occurred to me how odd this spectacle must have seemed to the Plains Indians still populating these areas and sitting in those classrooms. I think about things like that now, in a way I didn't then. The thing I did think about then—the thing I was obsessed with—was how much I loved to hear "Don't Let the Rain Come Down" on the radio. If you followed that up with "Dominique," you were all right by me. If you went on to "The Lion Sleeps Tonight," then I might just do the Indian dance for you, too. Life could be pretty hard a lot of the time, but when those songs came on everything felt good and right and safe.

G'DAY

⁊

As great as those songs were, I did not feel good or safe or even remotely right when my mom, just weeks away from her graduation at Nebraska Wesleyan University, decided she'd had enough of living in the roach motel with Paul Harvey's biggest fan. I'm still not sure what precipitated the event, but I do remember my mother's eyes and voice as she paced unseeing through the basement, constantly retracing her steps as if she were on a track. She kept saying, "I'm going to kill myself, I'm going to kill myself, I gotta get out, I'm going to kill myself," while looking periodically to the left and right for the yellow plastic braided laundry rope she knew was stashed somewhere in that house. She didn't seem to be aware of our presence, she was so engrossed and focused on the task before her. We tugged on her hands and her arms, imploring her not to do it. "Please, Mommy...Please don't pleeeeeeeeaaaaaaase pleaaasssse." I have never felt so invisible in my life as in those minutes of that day.

She did eventually find the yellow rope and she tied it onto an exposed pipe. She pushed a kitchen chair up under that rope, climbed onto the chair, slipped her head through the knot, and walked forward as if simply stepping off a curb. "Thank you ... G'day." That's what Paul Harvey would have said, but she wasn't Paul Harvey. She was my mother and she was swinging from a yellow braided laundry rope right in front of our faces, with her tongue turning blacker by the second, and foamy spit coming out of her mouth and eyes rolled up backward in her head. Lisa said, "Get up on the chair, Lauri, we can get her down, c'mon." In the end, my sister and I both climbed onto the chair—me holding Mommy up, hoping some air was getting to her, and Lisa trying to untie the knot, both of us screaming, until Mrs. Makosky and some other folks came running down the stairs. Mrs. Makosky was having an open house upstairs for parents of her day-care charges and our cries had completely annihilated any Norman Rockwell moments they may have been having.

The next thing I remember is a kind and matronly white woman squatting down and enveloping me and Lisa in her arms, trying to reassure us that our mother would be all right. A neighbor named Sally Rutledge took us to her house and proposed we all have a "nice picnic" to unwind and put our big day behind us. Her three kids were racing about, ecstatic to be having this impromptu hot dog orgy, but Lisa and I could only stare flatly into the sand at our feet. What could you say to anyone or to each other when a couple of hours ago your mom had been swinging way higher than you ever had on your playground swings, in living color in the little corner of the world you called home. My arms were heavy, my legs were heavy, my head was heavy, my hair was heavy. That night, as Sally put us to bed on pallets on her daughter's floor, she told us that our mother was very sick, and no one knew whether she'd be able to come back and be with us again. Lisa asked which way Mrs. Makosky's house was from where we were facing. Sally thought about it a second and said, "It's this way," pointing straight ahead of her in the same direction Lisa and I were looking. Lisa then turned herself around to be facing the other direction. After that day she always had to know where Mrs. Makosky's house was from wherever we were living so she could face the other way.

We were with the Rutledges for I don't know how long, maybe days, maybe weeks. At some point we got moved to some other neighbors. We were absolutely nuts about the Eaglestaffs, Bill and Lois, and their two boys, Danny and Tommy. They were just plain old good people. Bill worked at Nebraska Wesleyan University. He was a soft-spoken, patient, and gentle man who sometimes threw Lisa and me into the air perilously close to the ceiling, or rubbed his rough whiskers on our faces, making us squeal and shriek with delight. Growing up in an all-girl household with a mom teetering on the edge, we saw this as the father of all thrills.

The only downside I can recall while staying with them was all the powdered milk they drank. I can still feel my gorge rise when I see that devil girl's smiling face on that box of flaked hell that we had to choke down with our cereal and lunches. I can imagine the photographer putting a Hershey bar in front of the girl to make her smile like that, because it sure wasn't the Carnation Instant Milk that filled that child with rapture.

The Eaglestaffs went out of their way to show us love and give us comfort. Danny and Tommy were smart and funny and had enviable toys. They had an Erector Set, a couple of Slinkies, and a fire truck pedal car that they didn't mind sharing at all. Their uncle Itch lived out in the country with horses and donkeys and hay bales and trees and sky and grass for days. Visiting his farm was like going to heaven without having to die. He hitched his donkeys, Jennifer and Clementine, up to a wagon one at a time and gave us all a ride around the farm. The trip came to an abrupt end when Jennifer went one way around a tree and Clementine went the other, and Uncle Itch couldn't get them to back up and go around the tree together. We all laughed so hard we were crying, including Uncle Itch, and it seemed like the most perfect day of my life.

It soon became apparent to me that Lisa and I weren't going to get to stay at the Eaglestaffs' forever, no matter how much we wanted to. Things like eating lunch outside at their picnic table and making jokes with Danny and Tommy were becoming a routine we hoped would never end. A gnat would land in my powdered milk, and Lois would laugh and say, "He won't drink much, Lauri, go ahead and finish it." That struck me as the funniest thing I'd ever heard. So funny that I would drink it, and hardly even gag sometimes.

I loved Lois. After school we got to put "Fizzies" in a glass of water and the glass would turn purple and bubble and foam and hiss as we drank it down. Kool-Aid, meat loaf, SpaghettiOs, Lucky Charms, pork chops—while we were there we ate normal food in a normal house. There was tag outdoors until it got dark, Operation played indoors when it was rainy or cold. Our time there was a dream. It was a blow to us when after about a week at the Eaglestaffs' they told us that our mother was getting better and despite all predictions to the contrary we would be going back to her soon. The very thought of going back to live with my mother made my chest tighten with dread and fear. Lois told me that we were going to the hospital to visit Mommy and have dinner with her that night. She also said that Mommy might look and sound a little different because she was still sort of sick, that she had a sore throat and might talk quieter than she used to, but would otherwise be about the same. When we arrived at the hospital I saw that my mother had been transformed into a skeletal woman with black circles under her eyes, an enormous white collar around her neck, a dead stare, and an inability to turn her head from side to side without turning her whole body with it.

In the hospital cafeteria, Bill and Lois sat Lisa and me on either side of her, though I wanted to be light-years away, or at least on the other end of the table. I bowed my head as low as I could and stared at my food, terrified to be called upon by anyone to do anything. Silence... silence... silence. Like mine, the food on her plate remained uneaten. After some time Lois nudged me and asked, "Don't you want to say something nice to your mommy?" I could think of absolutely nothing, but eventually asked, "How do you feel, Mommy?" Seconds passed before she turned her entire body sideways with great care and deliberation. She swallowed painfully. I imagined tissue tearing as she finally whisper-croaked, "Fine." This interaction had cost me way too much, and I said nothing for the remainder of our time at the hospital.

POMP AND CIRCUMSTANCE

ⴰⵥ

This too shall pass. I've heard that saying over and again, and I think I've relied on it more heavily than others. For all the times that I felt swallowed by sadness and preyed upon by misery, a part of me wondered if somehow, somewhere, things would ever get better at home with our mother. We'd see glimpses of a better life when we lay in bed together, snuggled into her shoulders listening to her read *Puss 'n' Boots,* or singing "Frère Jacques" to us. Lisa and I both loved her, but did not feel safe with her.

Yet even when I felt all but certain that catastrophe and mishap would define our lives, I believed our situation would improve. I hoped beyond reason that my mother would become well and happy and that the anxiety and worry that overwhelmed her at every turn would cease. Lisa and I fantasized, often and out loud, that our mother's return would be characterized by the calm, nurturing serenity that we had seen from time to time on her better days. Gone would be the jagged, hyperbolic histrion who answered nearly every challenge with an action out of all proportion to the size of the obstacle itself.

My mother did recover somewhat, and somehow graduated that year from Nebraska Wesleyan University with a degree and a teaching certificate. After Mom left the hospital, we all stayed in temporary emergency housing while she resumed her studies until she had completed her requirements for matriculation. What a grand and glorious day that was.

Lois, Bill, Danny, and Tommy came to graduation with us. Lisa and I could hardly contain our excitement. My mother had a fresh scar— the imprint of the rope—on her neck, but you couldn't see it from where we sat. She looked radiant in the Eaglestaffs' Valiant on the way to graduation—her shiny black cap and gown so dignified, the swinging tassel hypnotic. It was thrilling to see her wearing lipstick and eyebrow pencil again and fussing over her hair. The night before she had methodically and meticulously put all of our hair up into a complex array of pin curls, which we'd slept on painfully, but happily, that night. This was to ensure obedient, wavy, perfectly coiffed hair for the big day ahead. The very sound and rhythm of her black leather low-heeled pumps clacking on the pavement that day was intoxicating to us as she strode steadily into her future.

What a long way we'd come from the day the ambulance came to our house a few weeks ago. For the moment, I was able to forget how hard the ensuing weeks had been. Going to school knowing my teacher and classmates had heard all about my family was hell. Lisa's teacher had even cornered her and asked for all the details. Lisa told her that she had no memory of it. Even at six and seven we knew this was something other than well-intentioned concern.

Nonetheless graduation day had finally come. My mother strode into the stadium with hundreds of her classmates—tall, confident, regal. A beam of light seemed to shine down from heaven onto her and only her. She was the most beautiful woman in the world. Yes, there she was, walking down the aisle to the call of "Winifred Jones" blaring over the loudspeaker for the entire stadium to hear. Oh, that was sweet. "That's our mommy! That's our mommy!" Lisa and I shouted. People all around us smiled and congratulated us. I could tell that they thought we were cute. Hell, we thought we were cute. We wore identical, frilly, two-tone blue-and-white dresses with white bobby socks. We carried white plastic purses in our clean, mother-manicured hands, and wore matching patent leather shoes. Red barrettes in my sister's hair, blue in mine. Our luck was changing. I could just feel it. We were going to be a normal family from that day forward.

SHALL WE
OVERCOME?

S*ure enough our luck did* change. My mother landed a teaching
job almost immediately after graduation. No longer a student and
a clerk in a department store, my mommy, I could now say proudly,
was a teacher at the Orthopedic Hospital on Fourteenth and South
Street in Lincoln, Nebraska. She taught English, grades 7 through 12, to
children whose injuries and disabilities prevented them from going to
"regular" school. My mother's job enabled us to do something we'd never
done before: live in a decent house in a mostly white neighborhood.
Thirty-nine twenty-four Randolph Street. Yes, it was a busy street; yes,
it was the funkiest house in the neighborhood; yes, it was sparsely

furnished with hand-me-downs and junk; and yes, it was all ours, and it was the nicest house that Lisa and I had ever lived in.

I started the first grade at St. Theresa's Catholic School under the tutelage of an elderly nun named Sister O'Shaughnessy. She was a tiny seventy-seven-year-old who often fell asleep during the day, and we all vied for the honor of helping her up from her chair. Sister O'Shaughnessy may have been ancient, but she had complete control of every child in that room at all times. We sprang to our feet when she came in every morning and chanted, in unison, "Good morning, Sister O'Shaughnessy." God help you if you were a boy who forgot to remove his hat upon entering the building. Girls had to wear veils to Mass every morning, and if you found yourself without one, a Kleenex would be bobby-pinned to your head in order not to offend the baby Jesus. Every kid in the room had about a thousand brothers and sisters and a last name like McCrory, or Sullivan, or Hannigan. I'd never seen so much red hair in my life.

It didn't take long for me to notice that we were the only flies in the buttermilk, or Negroes (as we said back then), in the whole school. It didn't take Sister O'Shaughnessy long to notice either, and one day she asked me why I didn't have better manners "like the white children," which annoyed me but didn't strike me as particularly offensive till I went home and told my mother what she had said. I told her I had gotten tired of waiting to be called upon because I often knew the answers before the star pupils (mostly the boys), so I had taken to waving my arm and hopping off the chair when I raised my hand. Sister didn't like this behavior, which is why she made the disparaging comment. My mother started banging pots around and muttering to herself as she finished preparing dinner. "I ought to go burn that honky church down.... Those goddamn peckerwoods better not make me come down there.... I'll give them 'nigger.'" My mother's display had shown me there was something uniquely different about Sister's insult. It wasn't anything like being called "slowpoke" or "sleepyhead." I was beginning to understand the word "racist" and that I would never be like the white children.

Aside from that incident, life was pretty good. By the beginning of second grade I had made friends at school and my mother still had a job. We still had a home, and at night, we got to watch *Julia* and *Laugh-In* and *The Smothers Brothers* on our first color television. I fantasized about my mother having her own TV show called *Wini,* and Lisa and I would be the adorable, albeit precocious, little kids. We'd say precious things just like Earl J. Waggedorn always said and our antics and dilemmas would be every bit as compelling as Corey's. It blew my mind that every week we got to watch a show featuring a colored single mom trying to make it in a white world.

My mom had a huge crush on Tom Jones, a white guy with an accent and an Afro. I couldn't imagine how he ever got himself into those pants he wore. He even kind of moved like a soul brother. I remember Dan Rowan and Dick Martin saying things like "you bet your sweet bippy" and Sammy Davis Jr. in his flowing black robe dancing around shouting, "Here come da judge, here come da judge, order in da courtroom, here come da judge." Flip Wilson's "Geraldine" with her falsetto "honeychile" this and "honeychile" that. Lily Tomlin's "One ringy dingy..." Goldie Hawn's hoop earrings. I did the boogaloo with Davy Jones and the Monkees as we all tried to cheer up sleepy Jean.

Bobby Kennedy was running for president in 1968, and Martin Luther King Jr. was leading sit-ins. Malcolm X was demanding justice "by any means necessary." I remember the day my mother came into our bedroom and told my sister and me that we were no longer "Negro" or "colored." We were now black. That same week she cut our long braided hair and we bought dashikis. When I wasn't wearing my blue plaid Catholic school uniform I was chanting "black power" and "we shall overcome" and looking remarkably like Tom Jones in my new Afro. The tables were turning so fast I had to jump out of the way. That week I went from the advantage of having "good hair" that was soft and wavy, to being consumed with jealousy over my sister's perfect, solid, kinky Afro. They say the higher the hair the closer to God, and by my estimation, my sister, Lisa, was halfway to heaven.

For the first time in our lives, things were good for us. My mother's attempted suicide now seemed like a distant dream. At night, Mom would come home and regale us with stories about "her kids" at Orthopedic. She told us about Fritz Matte, a big, blond, strapping farm boy of thirteen who had broken his neck while diving into a shallow pool of water to impress his buddies. Now recovering in the confines of a wheelchair, he was my mother's biggest challenge but also her greatest joy. He was angry with everyone about the accident. He hated that chair, and couldn't stand to be stared at. He'd gone from hero to zero in nothing flat. She had a gift with all of these children, but especially with Fritzy. Many years later I heard he'd been elected to public office somewhere in Nebraska. Maybe she'd been able to reach those kids because they'd sensed that, like them, she now found herself in a place she never thought she'd be, doing things she never thought she'd do. She didn't overlook or minimize their injuries, she just related more to their abilities than their limitations. She had an uncanny sense of how far to push them and when to stop.

She loved the English language—Shakespeare and Emily Dickinson, e. e. cummings and Edgar Allan Poe—and her love of literature was contagious. She would become so animated when she talked about Hamlet's dilemma, whether to avenge his father's murder or just let it slide, and Romeo and Juliet's families' feuds, that her students often forgot their trauma, if only for a little while. She drew parallels between the Capulets and the Montagues and modern-day racism and classism. She encouraged parents of kids who could travel to let them see *West Side Story,* as it was a contemporary version of the play they were reading in class. She knew there would be resistance to this request in the late 1960s in Lincoln, Nebraska, but she forged ahead anyway, asking parents to overlook the movie's apparent raciness or vulgarity in favor of the greater lessons to be learned. She abhorred provincialism and censorship born of ignorance.

She worked hard for her students and in return asked much of them. She didn't tolerate laziness or excuses. The students without use of their hands were outfitted with headgear that allowed them to tap out school papers using a pencil to hunt and peck on a typewriter. They were expected to turn in their book reports on time and with no spelling errors. She told us there was one kid so badly burned that he had to be isolated and confined to a sterile environment. His skin oozed and bled while she read *The Adventures of Tom Sawyer* and *Huckleberry Finn* to him. "What did Tom Sawyer accomplish by convincing his friends that whitewashing a fence was the most fun thing a kid could ever do," my mom would ask. "I don't know," mumbled the student, in obvious pain.

"Think about it!" demanded my mother. "Think about it, Michael. I mean really *really* think about it. What's so great about what Tom did?"

Michael replied, "Well, maybe it was like he was turning a chore into somethin' like . . . I dunno, like, maybe like a privilege—something bad into something good."

"Exactly!" my mom said. That's the kind of teacher she was. She got the best out of them even when they resisted. She told me once of organizing a field trip, a rare thing for her school. Somehow she arranged for a bus called a Sunshine Coach to transport all of these special-needs kids to a rally in Lincoln to hear Bobby Kennedy speak during his bid for the presidency. They were in wheelchairs, on gurneys, on crutches, you name it, listening to a guy who didn't look that much older than them talk about racial unity, the war in Southeast Asia, troubled times, justice for all, and healing. Mom came home jazzed about his speech. She couldn't say enough about the way Bobby looked and sounded and the way her students looked at him and listened to what he said. Mom said she was going to vote again for the first time since JFK had been killed. Things just felt good, hopeful, and filled with promise.

It was like an earthquake hit us the day my mom turned on the TV and saw the news that Bobby had been shot. I never saw her take anything that hard in my life. She ran to the TV and embraced the image of Bobby. She circled her arms around the whole set and wailed. She came undone; she just hit bottom. She kept saying, "First John, then Martin, now Bobby. No, God, please don't take Bobby. Please not Bobby. We can't bear it."

Lisa and I knew instinctively how profoundly terrible the circumstances were. And sure enough we were right. Bobby's death had been the pinprick in the balloon of hope that had been rising around us. She still went to work and continued to teach passionately, but ever so slightly things began to change.

The summer of 1968 was an odd time filled with a national self-doubt that was reflected in each and every one of us. Shall we overcome? Or can we just keep two water fountains, one for whites and one for blacks and be done? My mom said she'd never vote again, and my sister and I began to wonder if "Negro" was such a bad word after all. My hair even looked a little silly to me at times. Mom was easily derailed and often suspicious. The words "honky" and "peckerwood" crept back into her conversation. "Don't touch that, Lauri. These peckerwoods will think you're stealing it and put you in jail. . . . Yes they will. They'll snatch you up and be on you like white on rice." This student or that student would have "honky parents who didn't think their children could learn anything from a nigger."

Lisa and I stayed home by ourselves every day that summer while she taught summer school. We were told to stay inside and never open the shades or the door. Mom began calling home every few hours and asking us to open the Bible for her and to tell her the first time we encountered either the word "yes" or the word "no" in capital letters. We were not allowed to ask her why, but eventually we put it together that she was asking God questions, and he was "answering" her through the Bible and us. We dreaded these calls because although we didn't know the questions, we were painfully aware of her reactions to the "answers." It drove us crazy trying to guess what the answer should be. If we couldn't find a capital "yes" or "no" soon enough she became impatient and abusive. "Look . . . simpleton, it must be there!" she would yell into the phone. Or, "For God's sake read it, idiot. I can't stay on the phone all day. Are you sure it's a *capital* 'N'?"

I often wondered what her acquaintances and coworkers thought of her. She complained frequently of some perceived slight by her boss, Larry Sugarman. Once he came to our house when she first began working at Orthopedic, and I remember him as a tall, deep-voiced man with a pronounced limp. One of his shoes had a sole much thicker than the other. Mom said he'd had polio as a child. When they first met she'd loved him and gushed about his warmth and generosity. Now it seemed he took every opportunity to thwart or impede her at work. If she asked for additional school supplies he would say that the budget did not allow it, "while he gave the honky teachers any goddamn thing they wanted."

The same was true for a coworker of hers named Sheila Gowain. Sheila went from being a wonderful teacher and friend to being "that short little no-neck cracker" in just a few months. Sheila had been born with some sort of skeletal deformity that made it difficult for her to bend her legs when she walked and gave her unusual physical proportions. My mother began making vicious fun of her and justified it by saying that Sheila and Larry were conspiring to have her fired.

Lisa and I were threatened with bodily harm and abandonment if we ever discussed our mother's past with anyone. Specifically we were never to tell a soul, be it child or adult, that our mother had tried to hang herself, nor were we to entertain questions about our dead father. She told us she could not forgive us if we ever revealed our family secrets, and that we would have to fend for ourselves if we did, because she would be called home to be with God in the event of our betrayal. She would grill us on how to respond in the event we were required to fill out forms about our parents. "Simply write 'deceased' where it asks for your father's name. Your father died when you girls were very young and it's none of their goddamn business what his name was." When Lisa and I asked her where they'd been married and what his name was she would become irritated with us and say, "Oh, honey, I don't wanna talk about all that shit. It's just ancient history. Who gives a damn?" The truth was, Lisa and I gave a damn, but we knew never to pursue the matter.

In rare, unguarded moments she gave us small bits of information about him, which we held on to and cherished. My sister and I developed an uncanny sense about how to time and present a question regarding our father. It was best to cloak the question in a veil of indifference as we led the conversation from innocent queries about minutiae, such as, "Do you remember what our first words were, Mom?" or "Did we ever try to crawl out of our cribs as babies?" If we were lucky, and Mom was feeling lighthearted, she would be more inclined to answer a harder question, such as "Whose hair is more like his, Lisa's or mine?"

From this exhaustive trawling, we would sometimes be able to expand our body of knowledge about our father. We knew, for instance, that his name was Preston Love, and that he'd been a jazz musician who had played with Count Basie and Johnny Otis among others, and that she'd met him when she was a young, promising singer going by the name Wini Winston. She said that Love had actually been his stage name and that his real last name was Jones, which was why our last name was Jones, not Love.

We never satisfied our curiosity about what he'd been like when they were young and in love. We wanted to hear vivid details about their wedding. Who had been there and where did it take place? Had he been handsome? Did we look like him? Did he ever throw us up in the air and swing us around like Bill Eaglestaff and Dwight Morris had done? There was no end to the number of questions we wanted to ask about him, but knew we could not.

Lisa and I made up fantastic stories about their lives together, re-enacting our version of their courtship in scenes supercharged with adventure and romance. "Dance with me, you beautiful creature," I'd say as Preston. "I fear my heart would melt, were I to find myself wrapped in your strong arms," Lisa would whisper, girly and high-pitched. We'd imagine them racing along country roads in a convertible with their scarves whipping behind them, laughing all the while and finding it impossible to keep their eyes off one another. Our mother had what black people called "good hair," and we imagined her flinging it about in Preston's face as he fell deeper and deeper in love with her.

Then we imagined the wedding day. Legions of celebrities would be in attendance, along with scads of reporters, and you would hardly even hear the vows for all the cameras popping and clicking. All the papers would carry the news on the front page. The only greater joy than being together would be Lisa's birth. They'd both hover over the bassinet, gazing down at her. Dad would extend his index finger to her as her tiny hand grasped it and the whole room would be filled with warmth. As much as I hated that I wasn't there yet, I figured they were saving the best for last.

Life was just one big love fest until the asshole in the Chrysler screwed everything up. At least that's how we saw it. This was, we reasoned, why our mom was so nutty. She just couldn't live with the pain of her loss. It was all too horrible to have gone from Camelot to catastrophe so quickly. That's what we kept telling ourselves when Mom would call, yet again, to ask about the "yes/no" thing in the Bible. She even began calling the priests at St. Theresa's asking for advice. First Father La Porte, and when he lost favor with her, Father Roe. "I know God has a special purpose for me," she would tell them. "He may need me to join Him soon and leave the girls here." I can only guess their reactions.

At some point my mother became so convinced that God was coming for her that she packed my sister and me off to the rectory with all of our clothing jammed in a shopping cart, and our cat, Sugar Plum, tethered to it. We were to find Father Roe and tell him that we were in his care now and he would know what to do. I was only eight years old then, but I suspected that Father Roe would not know what to do. About three quarters of the way there, I persuaded Lisa to turn back with me and Sugar Plum and hope God had changed his mind about taking our mom. On the way back, we were overcome by embarrassment when an older neighbor lady stopped us and said we shouldn't be dragging our cat around like that when we played house. I didn't tell her we hadn't been playing house at all and that our mother was, at that very moment, probably en route to heaven. Instead, I convinced Lisa to turn the cart around with me, and we carried Sugar Plum home in our arms. When we walked in the front door, Mom was angry, as we'd expected her to be, but she got over it before long and dismissed the whole matter as an unfortunate misreading of the Lord's will. We weren't sure why God changed his plans for Mom, we were just glad to be home.

Mom began smoking her Salems at an alarming rate until her consumption reached all-time highs. There was always a dense blue haze in that house and Lisa always had a wracking cough. I was tormented with eczema and earaches, but to express any sort of pain or discomfort angered Mom, so we tried to appear healthy even when we couldn't breathe. My mother's own physical and mental health was so fragile that we worried that one more thing would push her over the edge. Her menstrual periods and the accompanying cramps troubled her so much that she would often lie in bed screaming at the top of her lungs. Lisa and I were so acutely aware of her cycle that we could almost predict the exact hour and minute that her period would arrive. On top of that, her excessive smoking would propel her into coughing spasms that often escalated into uncontrolled vomiting. Some days my sister and I would listen for hours, our hands pressed to our ears and our stomachs knotted in tension, as she moaned, screamed, coughed, and threw up.

I feared people could hear it from the street and that someone would break into the house and haul us all off to God knows where. At times Lisa's breathing became so labored that she could not sleep, sometimes coming close to losing consciousness. On one of those occasions my mother screamed at her to "go the hell to sleep, goddammit." After some time I could still hear my sister struggling to breathe in her bed, trying to muffle the sound of her own gasping. Without warning my mom stomped into our bedroom and tore Lisa from her bed and into an upright position on the floor. "I told you to go the hell to sleep and I meant it," she bellowed, yanking Lisa into the kitchen. "How dare you keep me awake on a school night, you little pig, how dare you do this to me," she repeated. My sister stood in a kitchen corner in her underwear where she had to stay put "the whole goddamn night" until she learned "how to go to sleep when she was told." When I was sure Mom was asleep, I snuck into the kitchen and delivered my sister a blanket, telling her I was sorry for her and that I hoped she'd be all right until morning. Then I went back to my own bed. Episodes like this became more frequent in those days and months following Bobby Kennedy's death.

HAIL MARY

Mom *became convinced* that instead of calling her to his side, our Lord now wanted her to remain on earth to perform his will. She told us that she was God's wife and that He had big plans for the two of them. This new role meant that she would need some operating cash, because schoolteachers obviously don't make enough to change the world. With her help, she and God would rid the planet of all its ills—of hunger, poverty, racism, disease, and war. To make herself more available for God's agenda, she either quit or got herself fired from the Orthopedic Hospital. I never found out what happened. All I know is that money was really scarce and bills began to pile up. The phone began to ring as people called demanding their money, often threatening to turn off the lights or the gas. Macaroni and cheese became a mainstay of our diet and meat disappeared altogether as we could no longer afford it. What little money Mom did have went to the cigarettes she could not live without.

Mom took to reciting continuous repetitions of the holy rosary, as it was necessary for her to achieve a "state of grace" through constant prayer. Lisa and I were also essential to the successful transformation of the world as we knew it. As Mom put it, "We all had to pray and pray and believe with all of our hearts and souls that the Lord would intervene to succor us in our time of need." The prayers would relieve the financial burden of providing for us while doing the Lord's work, reserved only for her.

Before saying each rosary my mother would ask our Holy Father *and* Mother Mary *and* the baby Jesus *and* Saint Jude, patron saint of hopeless causes, to deliver a check for ten thousand dollars by mail within the week. This prayer request was the most specific Lisa and I had ever heard, and we'd heard a lot of them at Mass every morning before school at St. Theresa's. We admired her pluck, though, and fervently hoped that our Savior would see it that way, too. Something happens to a person when they say that many rosaries day after day. A part of me believed that the money would appear. I remember walking home from school sometimes to find my mother still in bed with her Bible, alternately reading verses and dozing, trying to force time to pass until the mail was delivered. Often on those walks, we'd near our house and I'd glance nervously at my sister and ask her, "You think it's gonna be there, Lise?" She'd shrug and say, "I don't know.... I sure hope so." We'd walk slower and slower as we approached the mailbox. Then we'd just stand there looking at it as if it were the Holy Grail. I'd reach for it and then draw my hand back at the last minute. It reminded me of the way I'd chickened out on the high diving board at the pool the summer before.

Finally, the two of us would open the door and look inside, nearly sticking our entire heads in if we didn't see anything. As much as we wanted to panic at this point, neither of us did. We'd look at each other and one of us would say something like, "She probably already got the mail...huh?" And the other would respond, "Yeah, I bet she did." Well, sure enough, Mom usually had checked that box at least three times during the day, and sure enough, no ten thousand dollars. Another quiet evening lay ahead, if we were lucky. On one particular night, we weren't. When the check failed to arrive, Mom gathered up some of the God-abilia she'd bought at the church goods store with money we could ill afford to spend, and piled it into the kitchen sink with pages of the Bible ripped out and stuffed between the plastic Jesuses, Marys, and Josephs. She headed to the stove with a page in her hand and lit a burner. Touching the paper to the gas flame, she had the tool she needed to set the whole thing ablaze. Her face glowed as the fire licked the porcelain sink and the plastic icons melted and contorted, sending toxic black fumes throughout the house. Lisa and I stood to the side, fearing the whole house would go up in flames if she didn't quit adding to the growing fire. Just like when she'd tried to hang herself, she didn't seem to realize Lisa and I were in the room with her as she raved. "Jesus is a goddamn liar. He's just another honky with a dick. Fuck you, Jesus. Fuck you and your lyin' honky mouth. I hate you, you lyin' peckerwood pigfucker." I reached past her to grab the faucet, trying to douse the flames. Mom shoved me aside and I, too, became "just another honky with a dick."

In later years and calmer times Lisa and I would often revisit those days. I'd ask her if I could borrow a blouse or a pair of pants and she'd say "no" because she was going to wear them that day and I'd reply, "I hate you, you lyin' peckerwood pigfucker, fuck you and your lyin' honky mouth," and we'd both fall down laughing. God bless Lisa for that.

EIGHTY DAYS

❧

S*omething had to give* and eventually it did. Our landlords, Marvin and Maxine Koeppel, were beginning to rue the day they rented to the likes of us. I'm sure it crossed their minds more than once that the "shanty Irish" they were used to had it all over the "coloreds" in the disposition department. At least the Irish were friendly and offered them a drink sometimes when they came looking for rent. Not only was their relationship with my mother strained for racial reasons, but I suspect she'd neglected to pay them for some time. I know that our white neighbors resented us living so close because it pointed to their own slipping stations in life. Once I saw Marvin and another man tracing the sewer line at the property boundary, trying to locate the

source of a plumbing backup. The three of us overheard Marvin specu-
late that the problem may have been caused by a tampon clogging the
pipes. This remark incensed my mother, who felt she'd been accused
wrongly. She grabbed a butcher knife and paced the house, maniacally
glaring out the window. "I'm gonna kill me a honky before this day is
through," she repeated over and over under her breath, with the knife
clasped tightly in her fist. She'd not allowed the Koeppels entry onto
the property for over a year and constantly voiced anger and bitterness
over their maintenance requests. Our time on Randolph Street was
growing short and one day they evicted us.

Mom was now in a free fall, and our eviction commenced a year of
wandering that changed Lisa and me forever. I now liken it to the Peace
Corps or some other tour of duty in a foreign land that, while difficult,
built character and shaped us in ways we never imagined. Mom either
checked herself back into the Nebraska State Hospital or Father Roe
committed her. Nevertheless, Lisa and I soon found ourselves roaming
from home to home, family to family, trying to get through the year
1969. Before the year was over we had attended four schools and lived
in at least as many foster homes.

We stayed with the Delgado family first. They lived a few blocks
from St. Theresa's. The father, Manuel, was Mexican and the mother,
Corky, was white. They had two daughters named Micky and Lettie.
Corky also had a twelve-year-old daughter from a previous relationship named Khristyne. Khristyne turned out to be the sluttiest little girl
Lisa and I had ever known. She flat out amazed us with her sexual ex-
cesses. No matter what time of day it was, it seemed she was grinding
with some boy somewhere in the house. She didn't care for the two of
us and made no secret of it. She once told us that her mom had just
taken us in for the money. "She gets a check every month to put up
with you little brats," she said, popping and smacking her gum. "As

soon as she gets caught up on her bills you guys are outta here." Then she'd go back to thrusting her hips into those of her latest love, invariably a skinny, acned, greasy-haired white boy with a perpetual sneer and a cigarette dangling from his mouth.

Khris loved to surprise and impress us with impromptu illustrations of her acumen in the ways of love. Lisa and I had never seen such things in our own house. Our mom might have been crazy, but she'd never been cheap and we'd never really lived in a house with men. I learned what "French kissing" was from Khris, as well as "finger fucking" and "nigger lipping" cigarettes.

Corky would sometimes argue with her husband and these interactions often escalated into physical fighting. Manuel would come home late from the bars he hung out in after work. Upon his arrival Corky would voice some sweet nothing like, "Well if it isn't my fat lazy alcoholic Mexican husband." Then he'd slap her. She'd scream, and he'd slap her a little more. Then she'd bring out the heavy artillery and start in with, "Fuck you, asshole beaner jerk." She'd mock his accent by saying stuff like, "You're never gettin' another blow yob from me, you greasy son of a bitch." When he'd effectively neutralized her and secured the scene he'd move on to Khristyne, who would be yelling from her bedroom. She'd rile him up with phrases such as, "Leave her alone, you fuckin' wetback," in solidarity with her mother. He'd charge after her, slam the door, and do God knows what. Both Lisa and I tried to blend into the curtains and stay out of the way during these episodes, sometimes hiding in Manuel's mother's room.

Concepción, Manuel's mother, was nearly deaf and blind. She also had difficulty walking, and was what we then called senile. Corky resented having to care for her husband's mother in their home; the old woman was barely mobile, unable to speak English, and incontinent. Concepción's bedroom adjoined mine and to get to the bathroom she would have to walk precariously through the room I shared with Lisa. Every so often she'd get up from her bed, put on a housecoat, and toddle past us to the bathroom.

More than once Lisa and I observed plum-sized turds falling out from under her robe as she slowly groped her way through the house. Sometimes this would happen when Corky bathed her. I poked my head in the bathroom once, unbeknownst to them, and stared in amazement at the pendulous wrinkled breasts dangling almost to her navel as she stood in the shower with Corky's help. As Concepción spoke only Spanish, Corky delighted in making bitterly cruel comments to her in soft, gentle tones while she mopped her up. "Oh look, Mama, another shitty present from your ass," she'd coo. "Yeah, we gotta get in there and wash that dirty little twat of yours once we get those melons out of the way, don't we?" Concepción never seemed to notice one way or the other what was going on around her, but I often wondered if she understood a little of what was being said. Once, when Corky and Manuel hosted a party after church, Concepción walked unannounced through the middle of the room in her housecoat, looking addled and unkempt as hard brown pellets bounced gaily onto the floor behind her. Corky was mortified and tried to laugh it off, gently escorting Concepción back to her room. She later let Manuel know how humiliating the whole scene had been for her in front of their friends. Corky was self-conscious, if not outright resentful, about being the only biracial couple they knew besides Lucy and Ricky Ricardo. She wanted to know why they couldn't ship Concepción off to a home like most white couples would have done long before now.

Beyond the troubles with Concepción, the whole house seemed to Lisa and me to be in a constant state of turmoil. Homework was never done, the dishes never washed, clothes never cleaned. Despite all of our mother's problems she had never been a slob, and was often a better provider. For instance, Corky phoned the school during our stay, and told St. Theresa's that Lisa and I would no longer be eating hot lunch at school. She planned for us to walk home at noon and eat lunch with her and her younger girls, who were not yet in school. The first day we arrived to a dark house with no one there and no lunch. The same thing happened the next day. Before long it became apparent to me that Corky was applying the money the state allotted for our meals to pay off her debts.

Some weeks after our arrival at the Delgados' we learned that our mother was now residing in St. Elizabeth Hospital, another loony bin. We'd been told that her recovery from her "nervous breakdown" was progressing nicely, and we figured we'd soon be reunited. In the meantime, for some reason, the Delgados' foster-parent days ended and we were transported to a new home.

Uduak and Tashi Mbesi and their two sons, Chebbi and Cheechoca, were originally from Nigeria and still spoke their native language with one another. Tashi wore beautiful hats and colorful skirts and scarves. She spoke in a low but loud voice with an accent that I loved. Uduak bore exotic ritual scars on his face and drove a Mercedes he cherished. They seemed rich to us because they owned their own home, but they also seemed very odd. Tashi cooked strange foods and there was a unique smell in their house that came from some unfamiliar spice. We'd been there only a short time when Tashi gave birth to a little girl she named Nnonna. Lisa and I thought the child looked like a little monkey and we could not help but say so in private moments with each other. Tashi and Uduak were rarely openly affectionate or physically demonstrative with each other and there were hardly any emotions ever exchanged between them. Chebbi and Cheechoca spoke two languages and seemed unduly boisterous. We never settled in with them, but their household was much calmer than the Delgados'. It was a nice respite before our next stop.

From the Mbesi home, we moved on to the Graysons'. They were an extremely Catholic family who lived in an affluent part of Lincoln and had three children of their own. They were often performing charitable acts, such as providing temporary foster homes, as part of their commitment to the Catholic church they belonged to. Their neighbors were consumed with their lawns and did not allow their children or anyone else's to play on them. After all, there were parks for that sort of thing. I once witnessed one of them overcome by rage on discovering some sort of nematode wriggling beneath the surface of his newly rolled Kentucky bluegrass sod. This guy was wigging out and I felt uncomfortable watching him, as if I had walked in on an intensely private moment. His face was purple and every vein and vessel in his body was pulsing like a garden hose gone wild. This affirmed that we were no longer at the Delgados' or the Mbesis' and that the suburbs were a wholly different place from anywhere I'd ever lived. We liked Mr. and Mrs. Grayson quite a lot, but cared less for their children, who seemed spoiled and resentful of us. Our tenure in their home would be brief though, lasting only a few weeks, as our mother, with whom we'd had little contact, abruptly appeared to prepare us for our next move.

This meant Lisa and I were now sharing a room in the Graysons' house with our newly released mother. On her first night there, Mom noticed she'd gotten her period a few days early as she prepared to walk across the hallway to shower. She stood in horror gaping at her crotch as a clot of blood dripped from her body onto the hardwood floor. "Oh my God, what am I going to do? Help me! Help me!" she whisper-wailed to us. Lisa calmed her while I ran to the bathroom for toilet tissue. My mother could always turn common, minor inconveniences into full-blown crises. We're not long for this place, I concluded while taking a mental inventory of the stuff I wanted to take to wherever we were going next. I knew Mom had made arrangements to take us somewhere, but she did not seem inclined to explain her plans.

A few days later we moved in with an old black widower named J. D. Bowen. An old family friend of our mother's, he offered us shelter in exchange for cooking and minimal elder care. I'm sure once he tasted my mom's cooking he regretted that decision. She was not given to domestic tasks. It was the first time that Lisa and I had ever lived with an unmarried man, and we thought it might be fun. Maybe he would be like a grandfather to us. We were glad to have an outside witness to our mom's behavior, hoping she would modify it somewhat for his benefit. While she seemed to fare okay after her release from the hospital, she never seemed "with it" during this time, and Lisa and I were concerned. To make matters worse, Mr. Bowen, like Concepción, also suffered from a host of age-related difficulties, including incontinence and senility. Lisa and I knew he had problems because there were little Mason jars of urine lying around in every corner. The only bathroom was on the second floor, which was hard for him to get to unaided. He apparently forgot we were there sometimes and walked naked through the house. We'd never seen a grown man naked before and this was fascinating to us. "Did you see it?" I would giggle to Lisa as he shuffled past our bedroom door. "Yes, I think so!" would come her giddy response.

Just when it seemed our nomadic existence might end, Mom packed us up one morning and we left Lincoln, leaving poor Mr. Bowen alone to his own devices. Maybe she felt her luck had run out in that small college town and that there would be more opportunity, not to mention anonymity, down the road. Whatever the reason, Lisa and I found ourselves sitting with our mother in the backseat of someone's Buick, flying down Interstate 80 with our few belongings, bound for Omaha.

OUR LADY

❧

The old black couple with whom we had hitched a ride asked my mom a few questions and let us off in the center of town. Look at all the niggers, I thought. They are just like me. Up to that time we'd dabbled in negritude, but had never actually lived in a black neighborhood with black people. I thought to myself: I will hear wonderful music, sing wonderful songs, learn to dance in new and exciting ways, and wear colorful clothes unabashedly. We are finally going to have "the black experience." I can't wait. Despite the stark impoverished scenes of Omaha that greeted us as we rolled into that tired city, we were determined to make a fresh start.

❧

Our first order of business in Omaha was finding a place to live. My mother found a pay phone and called a Catholic agency she found in the phone book. I listened fretfully, as I knew she had little to no money. Lisa and I tried to gauge how things were going on the other end of the line and I put together that our mother was talking to some sort of church official who was asking her the nature and urgency of her problem.

She must have painted them an appropriately grim picture of our circumstances because they said that they were going to send someone to pick us up. A long time passed, maybe an hour or two, before two white nuns pulled up in a pink Rambler. They rushed nervously through introductions and asked us to get in, relaxing a little when we were all safely inside. My mother tried to smile while at the same time telling them we had no resources. They offered to house us for a short while until we found something permanent.

They took us to the mother superior at Notre Dame Convent, who extended a stiff, and not altogether friendly, greeting. Lisa and I were ushered into a dormlike room with two beds, and my mother left with the nuns. We spent the next three weeks or so there, and since Lisa and I were not yet enrolled in any school, we filled our days watching the nuns and talking with them as they cooked, cleaned, prayed, and prepared their Christmas program for the parish. They were "modern" nuns and wore reduced habits and headgear, so that we could actually see some of their legs and hair, unlike the Dominican nuns we'd known at St. Theresa's. We sang Christmas songs with them and learned to dance the hora as they sang "Havah Nagila" for a bit of cultural variety. Right around the first of the year, however, they told us they'd transferred our case to a social services agency in another part of town that "dealt with that sort of thing on a regular basis." Lisa and I roamed the convent halls and knocked on the doors of our favorite nuns to bid them a sad farewell. We weren't looking forward to leaving and wished something big would happen that would allow us to stay a little longer at Notre Dame. It was January 1970 and I prayed for a massive snowstorm. On the eve of our departure I fantasized about waking to a surprise party thrown for us by the mother superior, who, at the last minute, had realized she couldn't live without us and decided to adopt us all as the convent's unofficial mascots.

TWENTY-FOUR

TWENTY-FOUR

❧

There was no blizzard and there was no party, so the next morning we stuffed our clothes back into plastic bags, and were taken by the nuns to the Salvation Army on North Twenty-fourth Street, the heart of the Omaha ghetto. It was a wasteland of bullet-ridden brick shops with boarded-up windows and broken glass littering the streets and doorways. The main office of the Salvation Army was a mess, with a clutter of office machinery that barely worked, broken furniture, and grimy floors. The blackboard announced meetings like "How to fill out a job appication" and "Hot lunch programs for your chilren—enrollment deadlines." A government-issue poster on the wall portrayed slim and muscled black people in earth tones working toward some undefined common goal. I think it was supposed to inspire us to get off our lazy asses and try to accomplish something—anything.

"Y'all have a 'pointment?" bellowed the largest black woman I had ever seen. Her hair was shiny. It looked wet and was brutally trained as close to her scalp as was humanly possible. At first we thought she was talking to someone else since she was not actually looking at us. "I said, 'Do y'all have a 'pointment'—didn't y'all hear me jus' axe you that?" she said, louder this time and looking directly at us. Okay, well that's enough of the "black experience" for me, I thought. I wanted to turn around and hightail it back to Lincoln. This woman scared the shit out of me and she hadn't even gotten up from her chair yet. My mother, however, did not seem at all scared, only mildly annoyed at the woman's tone and presentation. Please God, please, please don't let her lose it now, I thought. Please don't let her start using all those college words and get all sanctimonious with this huge black woman in front of us. Please Jesus, please Saint Jude, please.

I was shocked and even a little envious at how calm my mother seemed to be in the presence of this hostile woman. Didn't she know the danger we were in? For the first time I realized my mom had known many more black people than Lisa and I ever imagined existed. We had hardly ever been allowed to meet and develop any relationships with our relatives. All I knew about black culture was what I saw on TV and read in magazines. The few black children I had met had been astounded by my lack of familiarity with the black community.

I began to notice how the other people in the office were looking at us. I thought I could detect a subtle difference between the way they looked at me and my mother as opposed to Lisa, with her darker skin. I took a closer look at my clothes, at my hands, at my legs and feet. I listened intently to the conversation around me and contrasted their loose-jointed rap with my own tight phrasing. I touched my hair and then my nose. I was having an epiphany, realizing that I appeared to these people, and probably to most people, more white than black—yet neither. As we sat in that office, my mother spoke in her usual style: clean, sharp, well-enunciated words delivered in modulated tones. As I watched them watch us her persona seemed affected to me, even a bit haughty. My mother was explaining that we'd just arrived from Lincoln, that we had no place to stay, little money, no transportation, and that we would need immediate assistance. She delivered this information more as an edict than as a request. We were in no position to be making demands, yet curiously, she carried herself like Scarlett O'Hara in *Gone With the Wind*. Embarrassed and frustrated, I wanted to shake her and shout, "For God's sake stop acting like Little Lord Fauntleroy. Can't you at least try to fit in, even if you don't feel it? Lisa and I do it all the time. Can't you see how much further we'd get if you said something like, 'Check it out, man, them honkies up in Lincoln is a stone trip—they done fucked my ass *all* the way up. Y'all, I'm 'bout to go *off* up in this motherfucker if I cain't get me some relief right now—can you dig that?'"

But none of that happened. Instead my mom stood there speaking the king's English to a woman who looked like she wanted nothing more than to reach into a drawer, pull out a gun, and shoot her dead. Sensing the impasse, a coworker, a plump coffee-colored man in his thirties, stepped in and said, "Looka here, Safonda, y'all done scared these poor folks to death, lemme see can I hep 'em with something— you jus' go back to your work." Safonda seemed only too happy to do just that. The man's name turned out to be Norman, and his whole bearing was so much friendlier that I had to resist the urge to leap into his arms and not let go. He told us that, although it was getting late in the day, he would see what he could do about arranging shelter for us for the evening. He made a few phone calls on our behalf, talking warmly and easily with those on the other end of the line. I liked the rhythm and flow of his conversation and the way he put words to-gether. Norman strung together phrases like "Right on, brother," "Sho'nuff," and "Lord, chile" in ways that sounded natural and un-forced. At the end of one conversation he turned to us and said, "I'm gonna hook you up with a friend of mine's got a house for rent. It's not furnished or anything, but it'll do for a while." He went on to tell us he was going to "write out a voucher," so we could pick up some groceries. He said if we hurried we could maybe stop at the thrift store and get some blankets and cooking utensils for the night. He drove us to the grocery store, where we picked up rice and beans and canned goods, and then to Goodwill, where we found some blankets.

On the way to our new house I noticed men sitting in doorways and alleys holding paper bags up to their noses, which puzzled me until I re-alized they were sniffing glue. Others had dark green bottles poking out of the tops of paper bags, which I learned was a beverage called Ripple, the neighborhood drink of choice. I later learned that in our new neigh-borhood Ripple was rivaled only by the soothing nectar called Champale. No one was freaking out about nematodes here. As we drove, Norman switched on the radio and hummed along to a soulful song that Lisa and I had never heard. He had a pleasant voice, which offset somewhat the unappealing sights we were seeing. The house Norman pulled up to bore the address 2424 Spaulding. It looked condemned. As I looked around I saw that many of the neighboring homes were, in fact, condemned. A middle-aged black man in coveralls emerged from the front door and walked toward us as we got out of the car. He greeted us with a booming voice and smiled broadly. Norman extended his hand to the man, and they gave each other what looked to be a secret soul brother handshake. I filed it away in my memory to learn later. The man turned his gaze to my mother and said, "Hi, you must be Miz Jones."

"Yes," my mother said coldly. I thought of the words of my uncle

Harold, whom I had been introduced to once when my mother was looking for someone to loan her money. She was badgering him and he had said, "If you're lookin' for honey, don't kick the hive." "Stop kicking the hive," I wanted to shout. We needed a lot of help, and being surly wasn't going to get it. My train of thought was broken by the man's deep voice. "Omaha Nebraska Morrow is my name. Omaha Nebraska— just like where you at." Lisa and I could not believe our ears, and since my mother was mishandling the social amenities, I ventured, "No fooling? Is your name *really* Omaha Nebraska?" "It sure is, honey—same as my daddy's. All my people have lived no more than a few blocks from here for generations."

I must have looked incredulous, because he laughed aloud. A hearty guffaw. Could it be that his grandfather was so enamored of this place that he named his son after it? An homage to Omaha. Maybe the place was different back then. Like maybe it didn't stink, and maybe there weren't bullet holes everywhere, and maybe they just used glue for furniture back then. Maybe "ripple" had been something the water did when a gentle breeze hit it just right. All I knew was Omaha Nebraska Morrow was opening the front door and escorting us inside.

Much of the front porch was rotted so I chose my steps carefully as we walked into the living room and my mom gasped. Great lengths of wallpaper hung from the ceiling, bare bulbs jutted from the sockets, and a brown, gummy liquid oozed from the walls. Lisa and I later named that goo "roach piss," because it smelled like urine and the roaches congregated near it. There was no furniture in the entire house. Omaha seemed proud of the place, and I didn't want to appear disappointed. He told my mother he'd cleaned the grounds up himself so we wouldn't have to visit the dump. Norman and Omaha continued to chat for a while, oblivious to my mother's stricken face. Norman wrapped up with our new landlord and then assured us that he could be reached in the office. They both turned to leave as I wondered where we'd call him from and how we'd get the dime to do it.

As soon as the door closed behind them my mother sat on the floor, put her hands to her temples, and screamed at the top of her lungs. Lisa and I were caught completely off guard and scattered into the bedroom. Norman bolted back up the stairs, onto the porch, and through the door. "What's the matter?" he shouted in alarm. My mother smiled calmly at him. "Nothing," she replied. "Nothing at all." Lisa and I remained perfectly still as Norman continued to stare at my mother, trying to read her face. They remained that way for some time, eyes locked. After a while, Norman turned around slowly and left. When he was safely in his car and down the road my mother, Lisa, and I looked at one another and broke out into inexplicable, uncontrollable fits of laughter. I was happy and relieved when Mom joined in and hoped this meant she was going to be all right here after all.

Mom soon set us to work scouring the neighborhood for cigarette butts left on the ground that had enough tobacco left in them to give her some pleasure. Back in Lincoln, we'd never done anything so base but we wanted to see our new neighborhood. We quickly found that few people on North Twenty-fourth Street left anything but the filter unsmoked.

THE LIST

T he next day Lisa and I continued to prowl the streets for smok-
able butts. I didn't mind, and hoped to pick up a few pop bottles
to surprise Mom with a little spending change as well.

Right away I noticed the number of dogs roaming free, knocking
over trash cans and littering the sidewalk. No one seemed interested in
finding whom the dogs belonged to, nor did the dogs themselves seem
to be looking for homes. Lisa and I had never had a dog of our own, and
we were anxious to establish a relationship with one or more of them.
"Here pooch, here puppy," I called out to one. To my surprise he came,
and Lisa and I started petting him. He seemed sweet-tempered, albeit
dirty and missing a few teeth. "Hey look, Lise," I said. "There's some

more across the street." Three or four more dogs made their way toward us. "Oh, they're so cute," we both gushed, trying to pet them all at once. They seemed starved for attention and shoved their heads eagerly under our hands. We wished we had something to feed them, but we didn't. As if they were transmitting some sort of telepathic canine communication, a dog here and a dog there picked up the signal and ambled into our circle until there must have been eight or more dogs hanging around us, all vying for our affection. Lisa and I were in heaven and barely noticed when a shepherd mix began baring his teeth ever so slightly at another who'd nosed in before him. We continued talking to them as our hands grew black from scratching their grimy coats. As they vied for position I heard an almost inaudible growl deep within the throat of a hound. Another dog quickly answered the challenge. The whole pack instantly erupted into a gnawing, gnashing, tearing, full-on brawl involving every last dog, with me and Lisa seized by terror in the middle. We struggled desperately to get out of the pack but every time we moved in one direction, the pack moved with us. Before it was over Lisa's culottes had ripped clean off, and both of us were filthy and covered with cuts. As quickly as it had started, the fight broke up. All the dogs simultaneously lost interest in the whole affair. Relieved, we watched them scatter and trot away. Neither of us called to an unknown dog ever again. We filed the experience into our growing list of things not to do in the ghetto.

The dog incident aside, the neighborhood was beginning to have some small measure of appeal to Lisa and me. There were an awful lot of other kids running around and we couldn't wait to meet them. Mom didn't seem in any hurry to enroll us in school so we just hung around the house during those first few days.

On my tenth birthday, January 5, 1970, we had a surprise visit from our two favorite Notre Dame nuns, who arrived at our house with presents. As soon as they got inside they reached into one of the boxes and pulled out a cake, shouting "Happy birthday" to me. They lit ten candles and sang. Then came the presents—two transistor radios! One for me and one for Lisa. Her birthday, in November, had passed unnoticed and unobserved. Now she was finally getting her due. Mom stood by with what could almost be called a smile on her face. Lisa and I were thrilled to have radios, especially since we no longer had a TV. We'd heard snippets of songs blaring from storefronts on North Twenty-fourth and couldn't wait to dive into these cool new tunes. The nuns could not stay long. They confided that they'd gotten permission from Mother Superior to visit us only after they assured her they'd be back in an hour. Ordinarily, she would not have allowed the trip to our dangerous neighborhood, but she finally acquiesced after they promised never to be out of each other's sight.

The best present was that my mother had found a new job. And, not only that, but Lisa and I were going back to school on Monday at the nearby Sacred Heart. My mother's new job, which Norman had found for her, was on the assembly line at a factory located down the street called Components Concepts Corporation, or CCC.

The job was increasingly imperative. We'd been eating a vile concoction my mother generously called barley soup, the mention of which had always made me nervous. Lisa and I had taken to dreaming aloud of all the foods we'd eat after her first paycheck. Sometimes Mom even joined in. Pork chops, mashed potatoes, cookies, green beans, toast, omelets, bacon, strawberry shortcake.

We also dreamed of the kids we'd meet at Sacred Heart, hoping some of them would be cute boys. We were just starting to think about boys in this way, in large part because of the Jackson 5, which was led by the cutest boy Lisa and I had ever seen. Lisa and I would lose our minds when we'd hear "I Want You Back" coming on the radio. We had never heard anything so irresistible—ever! "Let's never listen to anything else, okay?" I whispered to Lisa.

We met only two girls our age in Omaha. The first was our immediate neighbor who resided in the ramshackle house directly behind us. The youngest girl was one big-time ghetto-looking, ghetto-acting chile. She was very dark ("blue-black" as they said down there) with legs that were perpetually ashy and scabby. Wisps of nappy hair threatened to revolt at any given place on her head. Yellow snot caked her upper lip and hovered in a ball below each nostril. Tallish and bony, she sauntered up to me and Lisa where we stood dully in our own yard for lack of anything to do.

"Hey," she said, standing before us while she stretched her gum out and twisted it around her wet fingers before pushing it back into her mouth. Her hip jutted at an extreme angle as she wrapped her free arm around her small waist.

"Hi, how are ya, you live around here?" I responded enthusiastically, grateful finally to meet a potential friend.

Silence. She stared at me, oblivious to the fact that I thought she should still be talking. The girl who accompanied her also said nothing. I mean, "Hey" had certainly been a good start, but shouldn't it have been followed up with something like "You're the kid that just moved in next door, aren't you?" or "How do you find our little corner of the world?" I struggled to think of what I might say next. Both girls stared at me. Lisa, too, was silent. Eventually the younger girl offered, "My name Rochelle Monroe. This my sister. Whatchyo name?" Rochelle seemed to have an aversion to using the word "is" in her sentences.

"Laura," I said, warmly, "and this is *my* sister, Lisa."

"Huh," she said without energy. She then glanced at her sister, who to this point had not indicated any awareness that she was taking part in a social interaction. Her sister returned the look and an almost imperceptible communication flickered between the two.

"You wanna fight?" Rochelle said, to my undisguised horror.

Her sister smiled at my sputtering as I struggled to find words that might reverse the ugly direction this meeting had taken. "Um... No!... I mean, why would I want to do that, I mean, I just met you and stuff and I'm not even mad at you and as far as I can tell you've never done anything to me so why the heck would we wanna do that?" I said almost as one word. I could see that my discomfort pleased Rochelle, yet I hoped to salvage some semblance of civility as I began to retreat with Lisa back to our kitchen door. "Hey look, guys, me and Lisa gotta go now, 'kay? Mom's got dinner waiting and she gets mad when we're late, so we'll talk some more some other time, 'kay?" Nothing from them. Clearly they were disappointed.

"C'mon, Marilyn, let's go home," Rochelle said in disgust.

Lisa and I turned tail and walked at a clip back to the safety of our own house.

"Did I hear that right?"

"Hear what?" Lisa asked.

"Did I just hear Rochelle call her sister Marilyn?"

"Yeah, so?" Lisa answered, nonplussed.

"Well, then that makes her 'Marilyn Monroe,' doesn't it?"

We both threw our heads back and howled. At that moment there was nothing funnier or more incongruous to me in this world than the image of that girl who had just been standing before us and the lily-white, platinum blond, dress-blowing, "Happy Birthday, Mr. President" be-singing bombshell I knew as Marilyn Monroe. We smiled as we pulled the transistor radios out of our pockets and plugged the plastic speakers into our ears.

છ

Weeks had gone by since we arrived in Omaha, and Lisa and I now felt anxious to start anew at school. Our schedule meshed nicely with our mother's, as her day started a couple of hours earlier but ended at nearly the same time. Lisa and I were responsible for getting ourselves up and off to school while Mom worked.

On our first day of school, Lisa and I walked quickly down Twenty-fourth Street toward Sacred Heart, trying, as our mother had instructed, to resist looking directly at people as they walked by. On our way we noticed a large dog that had been hit and killed by a car. Drivers veered around the carcass without much concern. That would never happen in Lincoln, I thought. A dog that big would have been someone's pet. Surely it would have been missed and surely the "hitter" would at least make an attempt to find the owner or call a vet or something. Not here, though.

I began looking closely at the buildings we passed and noticed that many showed evidence of recent fires, shootings, and acts of vandalism. There had been race riots in nearly every major city the previous summer. Omaha had been no exception. Graffiti abounded, some of it rich and elaborate, detailing festive street scenes featuring wild-haired black men with busty women, all with large asses, smoking, drinking, leaning on shiny cars, and dancing. There were black fists raised defiantly in the air with the caption "BLACK POWER" centered beneath.

Halfway to school we came to a barbershop where a few black men were leaning out of the doorway, chatting and laughing. One of them said, "Hi, darlin', how you doin' this fine day?" and despite my mother's orders, I responded, "Fine, how are you doin'?"

"Great!" he answered, emphatically. He seemed friendly, as did the others, and Lisa and I were curious about what went on inside a barbershop. Noticing our curiosity, the man offered, "Go on in if you want. Have a look around. Ain't nobody gonna bite you."

Boy, was this ever breaking a rule, but we just couldn't help ourselves. There was so much activity in there and besides, we were early for school. "Okay," I said, and we both tiptoed in.

The men inside the shop welcomed us. "Come over here, precious, tell me your names," one of the men said.

We told them and one remarked, "Those are very pretty names, ladies. Ain't them pretty names?" he said to the other men in the shop. They all nodded.

Only one man appeared to be there for an actual haircut, and he was smiling broadly at us from the chair, as was the barber. I looked at the man with the shears, who offered, "My name is Ernie Chambers. This is my shop. If y'all ever get into any kind of trouble or need any help, you stop by here, okay?"

"Yes, Mr. Chambers," we answered in unison.

"Now, I mean that, you two . . . anytime," he said pointedly. "By the way, you can call me Ernie, all right?"

"All right," we smiled back as we turned to go.

"You Peaches' girls, ain't you?" one of them asked.

Peaches! I was incredulous. I had heard only a few people call my mother Peaches in my entire life and all of them had been in Lincoln. How had a barbershop full of black men miles away in Omaha come to know that nickname, which I had heard only a handful of times? "How do you know my mom?"

"Oh, we know Peaches," said Ernie. "Yes, we know Peaches."

I discovered later that the man was actually Senator Ernest Chambers and he was active in Nebraska state politics. But I never did learn how he knew my mother. The last thing our new friend, Ernie, did as we walked out the door was slip a couple of Tootsie Rolls in our hands as he said, "Bye-bye now." We walked on feeling a little safer, resolving to come say "hi" again someday soon.

∞

Sacred Heart was housed in an old brick building with an equally ancient church across the street. Though shabby and in need of repair,
they bore some resemblance to the buildings Lisa and I were used to in
Lincoln. The words "Sacred" and "Heart" conjured images of order and
decorum, which I liked, and I knew the school would provide the struc-
ture and routine so missing at home. Outside the school kids raced in
all directions, screaming and fighting, with no adult supervision, but
we knew that this sort of behavior would come to an abrupt halt once
everyone was inside the building.

Since our mother was at work at CCC, we had been instructed to
go to the principal's office upon our arrival to fill out the enrollment
forms, but before we'd taken three steps a deafening din assaulted us.
Boys and girls were running up and down the stairways every which
way without reprimand, and there appeared to be no hall monitors.
Not a teacher in sight. Lisa and I walked past throngs of children and
up the stairs toward the principal's office. Uniforms were apparently
not required here, which was to our liking, even though we had but
two or three changes of clothes apiece. It didn't look to us like they required textbooks either, because we saw none. We kept our eyes forward and our heads up as we scanned the halls for the familiar black
veils and wimples. No habits yet, but we kept looking.

As we continued to climb the stairs I felt something move between
my legs. Startled, I whipped around as fast as I could to see a much older
boy, perhaps an eighth-grader, with his arm up my skirt. "What are you
doing?" I started to ask as he withdrew his hand and ran laughing up
the stairs. Once we were in the office we saw a teacher arguing heatedly
with a twelve-year-old boy who was yelling back at the teacher, who
was yelling back at him. Unbelievable, I thought. What could they be
fighting about? It must be really serious. I listened intently. It seemed
the student had brought a knife to school, which had been confiscated
by the teacher.

The student shouted, "Where my motherfuckin' knife, man?...
Don't do me like dat, man. My ass done paid for dat knife. It mines, y'all
got to give it back to me. It mines."

The teacher shouted back, "Uh-uh, motherfucker, oh no you don't,
I ain't got ta give you shit, nigger, cain't nobody jes' walk up in this
school and act a fool whenever they want."

I had never heard a teacher talk like that to a student, and had certainly never heard a student talk that way to a teacher. The word
"mother" was almost always followed by "Mary" in my experience. Sacred Heart was not going to be anything like St. Theresa's in Lincoln,
Nebraska.

LESSONS

ᘐ

I was walked into Miss Davis's classroom by the principal. Both were black. This was the moment I hated most about going to a new school. When walking into a new room for the first time and being summed up by every pair of eyes, I always hoped to get through it with as little fanfare as possible. I hated being stared at while the teacher introduced me to a classroom of strangers who feigned benevolence while probably plotting what they would do to me on the playground later.

The only real difference was that here I became "that high-yellow bitch that acts like a honky and think she so cute," instead of "the only nigger at our school." Lisa had it a little easier that day. Her teacher and her new classmates had barely acknowledged her. Miss Davis looked at me with weary contempt. "Sit down over there," she motioned. I did as she said and kept my eyes on the board. She wrote out lessons—lessons I hadn't seen since the first grade, three years earlier. Some of the words were misspelled. In the first sentence we were to choose the most logical missing word from a list she provided. The sentence read, "My dog _____ away from home." The list she supplied was made up of these four words: "cat," "baby," "sugar," and "ran." We were supposed to choose a verb. Had I not been so ill at ease I might have laughed.

This has to be a joke, I thought. I ventured a glance around me and saw that most of the students who weren't still staring at me were looking at their hands or feet and not at the board where they were supposed to be looking. Some even had their heads on their desks with their eyes closed. Only one or two hands were up in the air, but I dared not add mine for fear of looking like a brownnoser on my first day.

Exasperated, Miss Davis (pronounced "Mizdavis" here) called upon a student whose hand was not raised and whose head rested on her desk. Clearly bothered, the girl roused herself and squinted at the board, trying to figure out what she was supposed to say. A long time seemed to elapse. Finally the girl said "sugar" laconically.

"How the hell it gon' be 'sugar'?" Mizdavis jeered. "Do that make sense to you?"

Had it been me, I'd have been under my desk at this point rather than sitting at it, but the girl just shrugged, seeming indifferent. None of the other kids laughed at her wrong answer. Few even noticed.

However, Miss Davis was not done. "I'm axin' you to look at the damn sentence and pick out a word that make sense, and 'sugar' don't make sense. How you gon' say 'My dog sugar away from home' . . . huh?"

"I used to have a dog named Sugar," she said defiantly, lips peeled back from her teeth, "and he gone now. Dat why it make sense to me. 'My dog, Sugar, away from home.'"

Sweet Jesus, I thought, we are never going to get through verbs.

That whole first week was a washout. One girl named Denise Richardson said, "Hi," and even smiled at me. She said no more after that, but I was grateful. Most students weren't hostile, just disinterested. Those who were hostile, though, made no attempt to hide it. They didn't like the way I looked or spoke: too light, too proper. One lunch hour I sat on a swing by myself and an eighth-grader named Carrissa Mattox came toward me, balled up her fist, and socked me in the eye as she told me never to steal her sister's sweater again. I didn't even know her sister and had certainly not taken her sweater. Another student told me she was going to "fuck me up" if she ever heard me singing in church again. Sacred Heart became a minefield for both Lisa and me. If I smiled at the wrong person, I stood a good chance of getting punched. If I failed to smile at the right person, I stood an equal chance of getting kicked. Walking past a group of girls in the lunchroom I'd hear comments like "She think she cute, don't she?" and "I'll kick that little yellow bitch's ass if she look at me."

My teacher, Miss Davis, couldn't stand me. She hated everything about me. My light skin, my wavy hair, and my extensive vocabulary were particularly annoying to her. Once, upon seeing a classmate struggle to read the word "achieve" aloud, I made the mistake of whispering it to him, thinking I was helping. Miss Davis whirled around, glared at me, and sneered, "Shut the hell up, didn't nobody axe you nothing. This is a 'A-B' conversation, so why don't you 'C' your way outta here." The class erupted in a chorus of "oooohs" and derisive laughter. I wanted to crawl out of my body that moment and transport myself somehow to any place but there. Another time, Miss Davis, who had detected my anxiety with long division and fractions, seized upon this weakness. In all the moving and shuffling I had undergone that year, I had failed to learn the basics of "new math" and had developed a math phobia. Miss Davis came to my desk and looked over the problem I was struggling to solve. "What, you cain't figure that out?" she smirked.

"No," I said quietly, embarrassed and feeling my face flush.

"Damn, you slow," she said, laughing as she walked away.

At least we'd gotten Mom's first paycheck, though, and it felt good to be buying food with real money and not food stamps. We began eating much better meals, no more barley soup. We were all grateful for that. My mother spent much of her time correcting our grammar as we picked up phrases like "That lil' heifer be trippin" and "Dang, she be stupid." The word "ain't" might as well have been "motherfucker" as far as she was concerned, and more than once she said, "No child of mine is going to speak like a hoodlum in my presence." That was more or less okay with me, and I continued speaking that way, just not in her presence. It did baffle me, however, how she could roll the words "honky peckerwood pigfucker" off her tongue so easily and still get bent out of shape when I said the word "ain't" from time to time.

My mother reviled her routine at Components Concepts Corporation and found the conversation of her coworkers stultifying. "They are so ignorant there," she would complain. "Nothing but welfare mothers and trash. All they talk about is their men and their goddamn babies. Not a one of them knows a single thing about literature or the arts or music or anything *I'm* interested in. If I even mention the word 'music' they assume I'm talking about James Brown. What in the world do they find so appealing about him? He is the most vile, vulgar, ignorant man I have ever seen. How could you get through your whole life without having read Shakespeare or Emily Dickinson?" she would rant. "One of them said to me this morning, 'Oh my baby, he pee on me. He love it when I come home and pick him up. Dat's why he pee on me.' For God's sake, can you imagine? Isn't that the most revolting thing you have ever heard?"

As I thought about it, having a baby pee on you, while perhaps unpleasant, was certainly not the most revolting thing I'd ever heard. And I couldn't say in all honesty that I preferred classical music to James Brown. I had listened to quite a bit of classical music with my mother, who played Schubert and Mozart, Liszt and Haydn for us on the record player we had in Lincoln, and I did enjoy it, but I couldn't see why it had to be an either/or kind of thing. With our new transistor radios, Lisa and I were hearing a lot of James Brown. Who couldn't like "Papa's Got a Brand New Bag" or "I Feel Good"? I thought, but I kept this thought to myself.

The work itself was mind-numbing. Over and over she placed minute plastic parts into tiny compartments on some product or other that she had been assigned to assemble. She performed this task all day every day. Ghetto work. Everything about that job and about the ghetto seemed designed to make you drink Ripple or sniff glue or do just about anything to get yourself out of reality. Every billboard on Twenty-fourth seemed to say, "DRINK, NIGGER, WHY NOT" or "SMOKE, NIGGER, WHAT THE HELL." I was only ten years old, and even *I* wanted to be all drunk and smoked-up. I feared my mother's job gave her too much time to think and worry and to become anxious. Then again, I couldn't think of any task or social interaction that would not make her anxious. I was anxious, too.

Somehow we did survive that winter in Omaha. School continued to be a trial, and our mother continued to hate her work, but we managed and felt we were beginning to turn a corner. We had a place to live, food to eat, and the Jackson 5 to listen to. Easter was upon us. In my three years at St. Theresa's, the holiday had always been a big deal, second only to Christmas. Sacred Heart, of course, would not be providing the same pomp and circumstance as St. Theresa's. There were no gold chalices resting on ornate silk tapestries, nor was there a grand pulpit surrounded by marble statuary and intricate fine woodwork. Great gaps and maws surfaced everywhere, bringing to the fore the overwhelming paucity of elegance that had been the essence of Easter at our old church. At Sacred Heart, the few stained-glass windows depicting the stations of the cross, usually the richest signature of any Catholic church, were either missing or broken. Absent were the exquisitely hued panes delineating the agonal faces of the eternally suffering apostles and saints. Blood the richest red, eyes the deepest blue. The most glaring omission here was the frantic, highly orchestrated preparation for the spectacular pageant and the inevitable packed house, decked out for the Sunday service.

In my experience Easter was the time when the church, school, and surrounding property were polished and decorated to the hilt. Shrubs were trimmed, lilies were delivered, silver was shined. The monsignor performed the services, never the supporting cast of priests. The parish's most reliable altar boys were chosen and their mothers fussed over their hair and hygiene. Hams were ordered, family summoned. Nuns and priests paid special attention to the lessons and sermons in the weeks leading up to the big day.

Sacred Heart, while not the best exemplar of Easter, did commemorate the occasion. A few lilies arrived, and a small measure of care had been taken to create an atmosphere of reverence for this most holy anniversary. The whole neighborhood looked brighter in those days leading up to the holiday. Our mother had not had a serious relapse in months. Moreover, it had been some weeks since anything truly awful had happened to any of us. No evictions; no dogfights; no sudden, panic-filled, late-night flights.

As the big day finally dawned, I was glad to see that a few parishioners had fussed over the occasion and were wearing their Sunday best. There were more people than usual at church, yet the Mass was far from full. Father Vavrina's Easter sermon was serviceable and not overly long. We stood, sat, and knelt with the others and took Holy Communion as usual. At the end of the largely uninspiring service, we filed out, genuflecting at the last pew and crossing ourselves with holy water before pushing open the heavy doors into the sudden flood of sunlight. Walking home afterward the three of us even engaged in something approaching levity, noting the talents of graffiti artists we found exceptionally gifted. I noticed Mom humming a tune I recognized from *The Sound of Music*. "My Favorite Things" always made me smile. Four or five blocks had passed this way when I became vaguely aware of a group of kids walking behind us. I did not think that I knew any of them, nor did I think they were particularly interested in us. All the same, I felt a creeping anxiety.

I didn't want to show any concern by turning around, so we just kept walking. And I knew that my mother's presence would discourage any thoughts they may have had of finding sport with us. Even in Omaha, most children did not mess with adults, especially parents. But then I heard what sounded like a taunt from one of them, a slur of some sort that had been directed at Lisa or me. I was surprised by the proximity of the voice and longed to turn around to get a good look. Louder this time, I heard the voice of a child whose message was hard to understand through her laughter. She was laughing so hard she could barely walk as she trumpeted the words, "You ain't got no Easter clothes, you ain't got no Easter clothes" over and over. My face began to burn and flush. My pulse quickened, and my body began to shake as I forced myself to continue walking with my sister and mother toward the shelter of home. None of us said a word, and I became acutely aware of my shabby, threadbare winter coat and my scuffed and battered shoes with the glued soles separating from the uppers. Our faces froze in horror, yet we kept walking. There were five kids in all still following us, Rochelle and her sister, Marilyn, among them, still jeering, chanting, laughing. Rochelle was the leader, but they all chimed in with things like, "Ooooooh, look at them raggedy-ass clothes they be wearin'—even they mama look rough. I bet they ain't even go to the Laundromat an' wash they drawers. They ain't even know they black, 'cept her," they said, pointing to my sister.

The serenade continued for over a block, until we were inside the house. Consuming, overpowering shame. Shame and rage. Absolute, all-encompassing, overarching hatred overwhelmed me as I made my way into the room Lisa and I shared. My mother continued to say nothing as she woodenly busied herself trying to prepare the ham and green beans.

How had this come to pass? How had the base occurrences and assaults that Lisa and I now found commonplace at Sacred Heart come to be visited upon my mother? Wasn't she, as a mother, immune to the attacks of children? Did any rules apply here?

My mother might be crazy, but she deserved to be treated better than that, certainly from this gutter trash. That last indignity was the final straw that sent me reeling into a savage place I had never seen before. That moment was more telling than any that had preceded it. Not my mother's attempted hanging, not my flagging faith in God, not even my slaughter of Jane's kittens represented as great a fall from grace as had that singular, sudden onset of pure, unadorned hatred. I was beginning to feel no longer like one who reacted to unfortunate circumstances, but rather one who wanted to create them for others. If I was not black, then what was I? If not gentle and kind, then what?

Later I looked out the window and spied Rochelle standing outside, apparently inspecting something in our yard. She sang softly as she gazed first one way, then the other, parading back and forth, flaunting her bright-red faux-leather Easter coat with its "fur" trim. The coat looked absurd. Rochelle was a troll. She continued her promenade through my yard. Eventually, she looked up at my window, and my eyes met hers.

I will hurt you, Rochelle, I thought, I will hurt you now, and you will stay hurt. I exploded from the room and out the kitchen door to reach her. I began to rip and claw at her hair and her clothing. I pummeled her with my fists, kicked her with my feet, and bit her with my teeth. I shoved her to the street and saw blood trickling from her nose and mouth. Tufts of "fur" and hair began to fall from my hands and onto the pavement. She was screaming. She was screaming like she was dying.

Her mother heard those screams all the way from inside her house, ran to her kitchen door, and began screaming herself. "Get off that chile, get off my chile," she screamed hysterically from the kitchen but did not come out. My own mother stood at our kitchen door. They began screaming at each other. I heard the words "yellow" and "bitch" as I continued to pound Rochelle.

My sister, who had been standing behind my mother, asked her if she could go outside and hurt Rochelle, too. My mother said, "Go ahead, darling. It's all right," and Lisa ran outside and into the street and began to hit Rochelle with me. Rochelle's arms were now completely out of her coat. That is how she got away. That is how the beating ended. That is how she was able to turn and run into her mother's arms. And that year, that is how I got my Easter clothes.

OUTRAGEOUS
FORTUNE

❧

I *would like to say that* my Easter attack on Rochelle Monroe sig-
naled an end to my troubles in Omaha, but it did not. She and I met
again on my way home from Sacred Heart two days later, and this time
I was not so lucky. Still sporting the bruises I had given her, she lay in
wait for me with her friends. As was our custom, Lisa and I walked by
the public school Rochelle attended on our way home. Suddenly we
were besieged by a band of kids, including Rochelle and Marilyn, eager
for retribution. Thankfully, we were able to sprint to the safety of
Ernie's barbershop before they could catch us. Ernie refused to let us
out of his sight until he was certain they were gone.

The next day, however, they found us again, and this time Lisa and

I were separated as we ran from them. Lisa got away, but I did not. Working as a team, the four of them exacted revenge. By the time I entered my front door several minutes after my sister, I had been beaten bloody.

"Oh my God," my mother cried, "what have those animals done to you?" I resolved not to cry and told her that it didn't hurt much. My mother ran outside to a nearby pay phone to call the police. Some time later two white policemen arrived at our house, and my mother told them what had happened. The officers conferred with each other out of our hearing and decided that they should walk the short distance to Rochelle's house and take a statement from her.

They came back a short while later. One of the officers said to us, "You say your daughter was beat up by her, and they say she was beat up by you. It really isn't up to us to decide who's lying and who's telling the truth. Basically, what you have here is a couple of street kids fighting on North Twenty-fourth Street. It really isn't a police matter. It's just a neighborhood dispute and people act like this every day in this neighborhood, so work it out and don't call us again unless it's important." My mother didn't say a word. She simply glared at them and they turned and left.

When they were gone, my mother told us she was "tired of living in this fuckhole where niggers acted like savages and the honkies that made them that way didn't give half a shit." She also said that since no one seemed to care, we didn't have to go to school anymore if we didn't want to. We didn't, so Lisa and I began staying home and listening to our radios all day.

My mother continued to go to work each morning, warning us to keep quiet and never answer the door. Despite our precautions, a man broke into our house while Lisa and I were home alone. We heard a rap at the kitchen door, but heeding our mother's warnings, we did not answer and hoped they'd go away. A second knock, firmer this time, was accompanied by a deep voice. "John, hey man, you in there?" I looked at Lisa and whispered, "Should we answer it?" "No!" she hissed as he jiggled the knob and called out to "John" again and again. We jumped out of our skin and dove into the closet as the kitchen door splintered when he kicked it in. After a few seconds of silence we summoned all our courage and cracked open the closet door. We were looking straight at a stocky, muscled black man in greasy coveralls as he scanned the room and assessed the situation. His eyes came to rest on our stricken faces as we peeked out. "Damn," he said. "Y'all got less than I do." He shook his head as he turned around and slowly exited the door he'd broken down minutes earlier. Once he was safely out of our house, Lisa and I burst into fits of nervous laughter. We could not believe that this man had retreated with such obvious pity and disappointment on his face. "Can you believe he didn't do anything to us?" Lisa choked out. "Man, we're even pitiful in the *ghetto*."

When Mom came home she looked at the door and asked us what had happened. We told her and she turned her eyes skyward and wailed, "When will it end?" Oddly enough it ended the next day when she reluctantly left us in the house alone again to trudge to work. Upon her arrival she was greeted by a throng of police cars and what looked to be a pile of broken glass and bricks where the front door had been. She asked a coworker standing nearby what had happened. The coworker replied that a bomb had gone off inside the building an hour earlier. At the time, I didn't know the motivation for the bombing, but looking back, it was no doubt race related. The tension in our neighborhood had been tangible in the weeks before the bombing. There had been numerous skirmishes with the police, one of which resulted in the death of a fourteen-year-old girl who'd been misidentified as a burglary suspect. A cop had shot the girl from a distance, not realizing that she was female and young until he approached the dead body. Components Concepts Corporation was either unwilling or unable to rebuild after that event, leaving my mother jobless and all of us on the verge of homelessness. For us, that was the end of Omaha. The next day, my mother collected her last paycheck and we left for Lincoln on a Greyhound.

Back in Lincoln, my sister and I felt happier than we had in months. Mom had little money, as usual, but we had an unexpected stroke of luck on our return. My mother, in her diminished capacity, had left Lincoln unaware that she'd been issued a teacher's retirement check upon leaving Orthopedic Hospital. It had laid unclaimed in some office for the duration of our Omaha stay. News of this windfall came as we sat in the Lancaster County Welfare Office waiting for assistance in locating emergency housing. Lisa and I had no idea how much money it would be, and neither did our mother. We knew only that whatever it was, we needed it and we needed it immediately. My mother looked at the envelope and opened it with an unsteady hand, while Lisa and I looked on as if our lives depended on it. Six hundred dollars and change. This check was more money than Lisa and I had ever seen in our mother's hand. It was as if God had sent this money in order to tell us that we were home now, that everything was going to be all right.

Mom cashed that check and we decided to forgo the quest for public housing and to hunt for an apartment instead. We found a furnished one-bedroom apartment in an ancient brick building called the Orlo, located directly across from the state capitol. The Orlo had originally been designed to house state legislators when they were in Lincoln. Although it had fallen into disrepair, to the three of us it looked like home. And so it was.

ETERNAL FLAME

I t *was clear when I* arrived at my classroom at St. Mary's that some-thing essential within me had changed. There were only a few weeks remaining in the school year, and I found myself again being in-troduced as the new kid, except this time, from Omaha. I looked around me with hostility and mistrust and tried to assess which of the stu-dents would be the first to threaten me. My goal was to not speak to anyone, students or staff, unless absolutely necessary. I just wanted to get through what was left of my fourth-grade year without trouble.

Therefore, I was taken aback when a group of girls walked up to me at recess on my first day and asked if I wanted to play dodge ball. One of those girls was Mexican and another black, yet the others, who were all white, did not seem to notice. This would never have happened at Sacred Heart. There, the races did not mix, and they called their version of dodge ball Smear the Queer; the game's sole objective was to throw the rubber ball as hard as possible and hope to injure someone. By the end of that first week, I had been the recipient of numerous acts of kindness. I even experienced a moment of unexpected popularity when I spontaneously recited Lisa's and my ghetto version of "The Itsy Bitsy Spider" for my new friends:

> *The eenstee beenstee spidah fuhgot to pay the rent*
> *He tole the landlord dat all da money spent—*
> *Here come da sheriff—he gettin' out his gun*
> *Now the eenstee beenstee spidah ain't havin so much fun.*

A star had been born, and I was that star! It was glorious to be able to go to and from school without fear. By the end of that semester, I had made friends of different races and socioeconomic classes, some of whom even had me over to their houses. How desperately had Lisa and I needed something good to happen and how precious was that spring of 1970, home in Lincoln.

My mother, however, remained unemployed during this period, and consequently, we lived all of that summer on the teacher's retirement check. Mom somehow managed to buy us new bicycles from Sears with some of that money, so we could go outside and ride and stay out of her hair in that small apartment. One of our favorite haunts was the Centennial Mall, a promenade featuring gorgeously lit fountains leading to the state capitol. It consisted of lushly planted walkways and water features designed to provide a pleasing backdrop to the capitol. During the day and on hot summer nights, Lisa and I would jump into the fountains and play, even though they were not intended for public bathing. Many a tourist and legislator tolerated our behavior and even found us entertaining as we splashed about in the water, fully clothed, and enticed other kids our age to do the same. An "eternal flame" honoring the immortal spirit of John F. Kennedy bordered the first of these fountains. When we felt particularly mischievous we would carry fountain water in our cupped hands to try to douse the flame, always in vain. We wished no disrespect to President Kennedy, we just wanted to see if we could put that fire out. We were always amazed at the flame's ability to reignite itself on those rare occasions when we managed to snuff it for even an instant.

That summer we received a respite from the chaos that had characterized our time in Omaha, and for this we were ever grateful. More so we were glad to be older now and living in a place where it was safe to roam freely outside of our mother's gaze. It was during the summer of 1970 that Lisa and I began to mend and trust, to become whole again and gather ourselves for whatever lay ahead.

THERE IS NO
PLACE LIKE
NEBRASKA

❧

A mong the qualities that made Lincoln such an oasis in the midst of what many perceived to be a dull and monochromatic state were its many contradictions. The bustle of the city lay in close proximity to the gentle Platte River and unimaginable expanses of fertile prairie. Lincoln was a cultural hub juxtaposed between wild grassland and domesticated farmland. Its large state university was a magnet for students worldwide who wished to pursue everything from philosophy and the arts to agrarian science. The college housed a number of libraries specializing in specific disciplines as well as art museums and performance halls. Lincoln was also home to working-class, boisterous, and sometimes downright obnoxious rednecks who came from the surrounding farms to attend school. They wore the title "redneck" like a crown, insisting it referred only to their undying devotion to the Big Red football dynasty. The relationship between "college types" and "rednecks" was often strained and antagonistic. Graduate students and other university affiliates were often seen by the working class as worthless "study geeks," whose only real talents lay in creating and deciphering wordy texts, which contributed little to the world other than to keep themselves employed. Rednecks, on the other hand, were perceived to be rowdy, thick-necked, jutting-browed, knuckle-dragging miscreants whose presence on campus was deeply resented. Every fall the "Red Sea" swelled on home-game Saturdays, as fans surged to the stadium to support the object of their affection: the University of Nebraska Cornhuskers.

How had I not noticed this before we left for Omaha? I wondered. Maybe I was seeing it so clearly now because we lived on Fourteenth Street, the main route to the football stadium. It was said that on football Saturdays the third largest city in the state of Nebraska was the stadium, trailing only Omaha and Lincoln in population. Nearly eighty thousand people packed that deafening house to its very limits on the occasion of home games.

My own feelings vacillated between embarrassment at the rowdy behavior of the Cornhuskers and great pride for our top-ranked college football team. The Orlo Apartments were smack-dab at the artery that served the stadium during the legendary "Devaney Years." Bob Devaney was the head coach of the Nebraska team that '71 season when they took the National College Football Championship. Bottle rockets and M-80s exploded throughout the day and night from the capitol to the university campus. Revelers overtook the streets in one long, drunken party that lasted for two days. Studies came to a halt and careers were forgotten as our little town and streets became the national focus for the whole weekend.

Although we had not been fans in days past, my mother, my sister, and I watched the spectacle with delight, first on TV and then from the windows of our little apartment, as we got a firsthand glimpse of unrestrained Cornhusker mania. That year the Cornhuskers capped an already 12–0 season by annihilating their bitter rivals, the Oklahoma Sooners, and then went on to win the Orange Bowl, defeating Bear Bryant's formidable Alabama Crimson Tide, which established Bob Devaney, in perpetuity, as the undisputed king of Nebraska football coaches.

LOOK AWAY

☙

That fall found my mother still unemployed, and when her money ran out, we went on welfare. I had begun fifth grade at public school for the first time since kindergarten. We had switched from Catholic school midyear when my much-loved teacher, Mrs. Lloyd, followed her husband out of state to pursue a better-paying job. Her departure, followed by the arrival of the self-proclaimed "Southern belle from Alabama," Mrs. Daley, triggered a rash of hostility in me that I'd never displayed to any teacher in any school I'd ever attended. With her pert nose and auburn "flip" hairdo, she bore more than a passing resemblance to Marlo Thomas in *That Girl,* which annoyed me no end. To use a phrase popular with my former Sacred Heart classmates, Mrs. Daley "pushed my nigger button." She seemed determined to bring all the traditions of her Southern upbringing to my fifth-grade class by teaching us songs like "When the Darkies Beat Their Feet on the Mississippi Mud" and "(I Wish I Was in) Dixie." The lyrics of these and other songs, such as "Jimmy Crack Corn and I Don't Care," made me cringe.

During American history lessons Mrs. Daley told us how slavery had been "a really good thing for Negroes" (pronounced "niggras"), because they were "childlike and unable to care for themselves" without the humane oversight of white people, "who took very good care of them—better, often, than their own livestock." After our time in Omaha, experiencing firsthand the result of that "humane" treatment, I took offense at her teachings.

Much of my outrage and hyperawareness of racism was fueled by my mother's disgusted reactions to Mrs. Daley's lessons, which she would often ask me to describe. When I refused to join in activities that I found offensive, particularly when we were asked to sing certain songs, Mrs. Daley demanded that I participate fully in the exercise or be sent to the principal. I would continue to refuse, sneering, "I'm not about to sing that stupid crap." She again threatened to send me to the office. Our principal, Sister Eleanor, scared the hell out of me and so, in a complete reversal of my original stance, I decided to comply. I did so by leaping on top of the piano Mrs. Daley had been playing and performing an exaggerated minstrel version of "Dixie" for the benefit of the entire class. I lost my mind when the room erupted into a clapping, screaming, cheering, gesticulating mob of delighted supporters. Every student in the room was shouting and egging me on as my performance got bigger and wilder with every hoot and holler. Unable to restore order, Mrs. Daley ran from the classroom, calling frantically for Sister Eleanor.

Sister Eleanor threw open the door only to find thirty-four cherubic fifth-graders sitting quietly at their desks with their hands folded, myself included. There were tears in Mrs. Daley's eyes as she sputtered her way through explanations to Sister, singling me out as the instigator of the crime. Sister Eleanor, who herself had been a teacher for a long time, found no humor in my antics and promptly escorted me to her office and expelled me.

For the first time in my life, I had been dismissed from school for disciplinary reasons. I was devastated. I had formed deep attachments to my classmates by this time and wanted to stay at St. Mary's, despite Mrs. Lloyd's departure. Sister Eleanor asked for an apology, which I submitted immediately and sincerely. She then asked for an explanation, which I lamely proffered, stammering, "I d-don't know why I did it." I *didn't* know what had come over me and deeply regretted having led everyone into such a frenzy. She picked up the phone on her desk and asked for a number where my mother could be reached. I told her we had no phone in our home, desperately hoping to stop the progression of events that was unfolding before me. She located my file and looked up my address. Noting how close I lived, she asked her assistant, Miss O'Malley, to walk across the street to our apartment to talk to my mother. I considered suicide as I looked through Sister Eleanor's office window and watched my mother emerge from the front door of the Orlo with the principal's assistant. When they reached the office, Sister Eleanor had my mother sit as she told her what had happened in Mrs. Daley's classroom. My mother then surprised me by asking me to describe in my own words what had taken place that afternoon. I gave her my version of the incident, taking special care to enunciate the lyrics of the songs I found most offensive. Mom listened quietly as I recounted the events leading to my performance that day. After I finished, she turned her gaze to Sister Eleanor. "You goddamn honkies got what you deserved," she said evenly. "Send Lisa home, too, I'm not having her listen to you vile, peckerwood curs another instant."

My brain nearly exploded with the shock of what I had just heard my mother say to Sister Eleanor. I struggled to comprehend what it meant as my mother abruptly rose and walked out of Sister Eleanor's office to wait for my sister. I followed closely behind, and we stood in silence as we watched Miss O'Malley scramble down the hallway to fetch Lisa. A few minutes later my sister came walking down the hall alone. I will always wonder if Sister Eleanor knew what the word "cur" meant.

INTO THE PUBLIC

L isa wanted even less than I to leave St. Mary's and blamed me for
our hasty departure. Though I was amazed and relieved that my
mother had not been angry with me, I was awash with gloom at the
prospect of leaving Catholic school and entering what we believed to
be an inferior public school system. I shuddered at the prospect of
walking into yet another new classroom in the middle of a school year.
How could I have fucked things up so badly? I wondered, cursing myself over and over again. I had finally found a school I liked and I blew
it. I resigned myself to the notion that whatever misfortunes befell us
at our new school would be my fault.

At the Clare McPhee Laboratory School, I was impressed by the modernity of my new classroom. There was fresh paint, new carpet, unmarred furniture, and mirrors all around. Textbooks were current and abundant. I was curious as to why the word "Laboratory" came after "McPhee" and before "School," but dismissed it as something I would ask someone about later. A tall, plump, grandmotherly white woman with huge eyeglasses stood at the board writing out an exercise for the class to complete. All eyes turned toward me as I stood at the door waiting to be introduced. Here we go again, I thought.

"Hello, Laura," said the woman standing at the board. "My name is Mrs. Gilliland. Welcome to our class."

"Thank you," I mumbled as she escorted me to a seat at one of the long tables arranged in a horseshoe configuration around the room. Each table sat six kids and contained a row of individual metal cubbyholes beneath to store tablets and pencils. I marveled at how any classroom could exist without desks.

Mrs. Gilliland explained that there would be a group of university students coming to observe us during our reading lesson at twelve-thirty. How odd, I thought. I wasn't sure what she meant by "observe," but I didn't think I'd like it. Intrigued, I waited through the entire afternoon for the college students to arrive and was unable to concentrate on anything else. I didn't know any of my classmates yet, so I couldn't ask if their being so late was typical. They never did show up, which was a disappointment to me.

As Lisa and I walked home that afternoon, she recounted a similar story about a group of students who'd been scheduled to visit, then failed to appear. Our initial impression of public school was that it wasn't so bad after all. The kids seemed relatively civilized and not particularly anxious to do us harm, and the lessons, while a good deal easier than in Catholic school, were just challenging enough to keep our attention. These two observations allowed us to overlook the fact that Clare McPhee had such a hard time coordinating visits with university students. The days passed into weeks, marked by my acquisition of a reasonable number of friends and allies.

One classmate, Jodie Weitzman, became my best friend and confidante. Once, while Jodie and I sat together at recess, I remarked on how useless it was for Mrs. Gilliland to keep scheduling visits with university students who never showed up. I thought it was silly to continue making announcements for appointments that were never kept. "I mean, she's old but she's not senile yet. How many times is she gonna fall for that stupid trick before she realizes they're *never* coming?" Jodie looked at me incredulously and asked if I was kidding. "No, I mean, don't you think it makes her look like a retard? I dare you to name one time they ever showed up."

"Well gee, Laura, ummm . . . they *always* show up" was her swift response. "Haven't you ever noticed all those mirrors on the walls?"

"Well, yeah I guess so," I replied, confused.

"They're two-way mirrors, you dipshit!" she blurted.

"Huh?" I said, still not getting it.

"You know, two-way mirrors, the kind that's a mirror on one side and a window on the other. The observers from the U always show up, you just can't see them; but they can see you!"

I was flabbergasted. "Do you mean to tell me that all this time, we've been stared at and I didn't even know it?"

"Bingo!" sang Jodie, gleefully.

I was overcome with panic as I tried to recall everything I had done in those last few months that would cause embarrassment. Could I possibly have picked my nose or scratched my butt right there in front of them? I remembered one time while taking a test, I copied from my neighbor's paper because my own answer felt wrong. I'd craned my neck to its full length as I peered over her shoulder. The only person I thought I had to worry about was Mrs. Gilliland. It must have been a regular laugh riot for the observers to watch me furiously changing my answer as I nervously monitored my teacher's whereabouts. I probably even walked up to the glass once to inspect a pimple with them doubled over on the other side. I continued to enjoy my classes and new-found friends at our laboratory school, but from that day forward, I conducted myself as if on camera. Those students at Clare McPhee had it all over me for being able to ignore the eyes behind the mirrors.

BEHIND
THE DOOR

⌘

M y fifth- and sixth-grade years passed quickly. Lisa and I began wearing pants to school for the first time in our lives. No more uniforms, no more dresses. I was twelve years old, sporting an Afro, and flaunting a pair of magenta bell-bottoms that I hardly ever took off.

Never mind the caustic remarks from my mother at home when she'd tear open the latest "Get out there and get a job" letter from the welfare agency. "I don't give a shit what those crackers do to me," she'd spit. "I've got a plan for them, too." I dreaded summer, when I knew we'd be seeing a lot more of her, which wouldn't be good for any of us.

On the last day of school, Jodie Weitzman walked me halfway home, as was her custom, before splitting off to head south to her own home. We promised to see each other as much as we could over vacation, and I hoped we would. When I got inside the house that cloudless June day, my mother was sitting at the kitchen table, muttering to herself, chain-smoking Salems, the Bible wide open before her. I was a few feet away changing into a pair of shorts to prowl the capitol grounds when there was a knock at the door. Mom looked up but didn't make a sound. I heard what sounded like a man shifting from foot to foot on the creaky floorboards outside the front door. After thirty seconds or so of intermittent knocking a male voice called out, "Mrs. Jones, I know you're home, and we need to talk about the loan payment."

Somehow Mom had obtained a two-thousand-dollar loan from Dial Finance some years earlier to consolidate her debts. I don't know how far in arrears she had gotten, but I was sure the man at the door could tell us. He continued to knock and speak firmly to us through the door. "I know you're in there, and if I have to I can get the manager to open the door and let me in since he says you're not paying your rent either. You might as well just let me in."

These words elicited what looked like homicidal rage in my mother's eyes. She tiptoed to the cupboard and produced a long pair of scissors, which she grasped tightly in her left hand. "Get the fuck away from me, you goddamn peckerwood," she roared.

"Ma'am, I can't leave until I get a payment from you," insisted the voice behind the door.

My mother glared at it as if it had done the speaking. We heard what sounded like keys jingling at the lock, which prompted Mom to fling open the door and lunge at the man with her scissors held high, screaming, "Get off my door, honky pigfucker! I'll kill you—just try me, motherfucker, you think I won't!"

The man pitched backward, ill-fitting polyester suit and all, narrowly avoiding getting stabbed, as he ran to his car, papers flying everywhere, yelling back over his shoulder, "I'm calling the police. You'll be hearing from us!" My mother stood just outside the threshold, scissors still raised, eyes wild, breathing hard.

I hung back by the sofa as she slowly came back into the apartment. "I'll kill us all before I let another white man take me away," she said flatly. I fervently hoped she was exaggerating as I pulled on my shorts and headed out on my bike. I was uneasy thinking about the words "kill us all," and tried to dismiss them as I looked for pop bottles, hoping a bit of change would lift my mother's spirits. I ran into Lisa during my forage and told her it would be a good idea to hang outside for a while until Mom cooled down. I detailed the latest debt-collector episode, the worst I'd seen thus far. We searched for bottles together, cashed them in, and headed home with fifty cents.

PERCHANCE
TO DREAM

⌘

That man never did call the police and I never saw him again, but our financial woes did not abate. For the most part, Lisa and I just stayed out of the apartment and hoped things would change. That June my mother began taking an inordinate interest in my dreams. I mentioned to her one morning that I'd had a fitful sleep. She asked casually what I had dreamed and I described to her the three of us sitting in a tree on the capitol grounds waiting for the water to recede from a flood that had moved in the night before. The three of us had sat like chimpanzees, watching the world float by as the water receded. She questioned every detail of the dream and asked pointedly if there had been any lights or voices in it. I told her that I thought not. She was perturbed by my answer. She asked again if I remembered any candles, moonlight, or whispers. Again, I said, no.

"Think, Lauri, think. Were there any lights or voices coming from anywhere at any time in that dream?"

"No!" I answered emphatically, hoping to end it. She seemed, for the moment, satisfied, and let me go outside for the day.

I hadn't felt great all morning but preferred being outdoors to being trapped inside with my mother. A few hours later, sitting back on the stoop of the Orlo, I looked down and thought I'd been cut somehow playing in the sprinklers. Blood was running down the inside of my legs past the yellow shorts I'd been wearing. "Oh no," I said to Lisa. "I think I hurt myself."

She inspected the "injury" and scoffed, "Don't you know what that is?"

"Ohhhhhh . . ." I finally got it. "My period." Lisa had started hers the year before, and I was glad she knew what to do.

"We need to go inside right now and find the Kotex," she said knowingly.

"Okay." We went indoors and Lisa excitedly told my mother that I'd started my period.

"Oh great," my mother said sarcastically. "Now we can go broke buying more rags." I knew very little about my own anatomy as my mother had always been prudish and hated talking about anything of a sexual nature. She could say the words "pigfucker" and "honky with a dick" without skipping a beat, but she refused to answer any physiological queries we might have, especially if they were about the terrifying region she referred to as "down there." I knew what cramps were because I'd heard my mother wailing every month from her bed, but other than a little discomfort, I didn't feel that bad myself. Lisa showed me how to put on the contraption known as the Modess Belt, which consisted of an elastic waistband with tabs hanging down front and back, each holding a plastic triangular catch with tiny metal teeth. The teeth held the mattress-sized napkin in place. There were no such things as "wings" or "adhesive strips" back then, and I felt like a giant baby wearing something that so resembled a diaper. Harnessed and prepared for the worst, I headed for the door in clean, dark shorts that I hoped would hide the bulky pad.

On my way out the door, Mom stopped me and said, "Now, Lauri, tell me again about the flood." I was irritated as hell to be stopped yet again and told to recount my stupid dream so I began adding things that I thought would placate her and tide her over for a while. I said things like "Now I remember, there were crows everywhere, and they were able to talk and said 'come this way' to us. And that's how we knew how to avoid the deep water and not drown." What I hoped would be the conclusion of my tale sparked my mother's curiosity, and instead of being satisfied, she asked for more. By the time she released me, I'd woven such a tangled web I couldn't remember what I'd said.

Lisa and I sat on the stone steps of the capitol as we tried to figure out what had gotten into our mother this time. Whatever it was, it was better than anger, or despondence, and for that we were cautiously grateful. The next few mornings my mother sat at the table smoking and peered at us through the doorway, waiting for Lisa and me to wake up. Her Bible lay before her as she alternated between staring at us and checking for Yeses and Nos.

On one such morning just before dawn, I became aware of a voice whispering above me. Instinctively I resisted the urge to sit up to see what was happening. Instead, I lay quietly, eyes open a slit, and maintained my deep rhythmic breathing as if still asleep. I could just make out the shape of my mother kneeling on the floor beside me where I lay on a pallet in the living room. She seemed to be having a conversation with someone, yet no one besides Lisa was in the room. "Mother Mary, give me the strength to carry out your will," she prayed. "I can't do it without your help, Jesus. Please help me, Mary, please."

As I listened I was able to glean that my mother was "communicating" with Mother Mary and the Holy Trinity: God the Father, God the Son, and God the Holy Ghost—as well as some of the saints. She was asking for their help to do something that she found quite difficult. What was it? I wondered, but continued to feign sleep. Her pleading continued for some time until she finally got up and walked into her bedroom, saying, "I'm sorry. I just can't do it without your help," and closed the door behind her.

I looked at my sister, who was also listening. She had been lying on the couch a foot away and from her vantage point could see that my mother had held an extension cord suspended over my head as she spoke. Lisa said she'd been compulsively pulling it taut, then slackening it as if to test its strength, as she whispered above me.

Lisa and I rose from our beds, folded and put away our bedding, and headed for the capitol. Later that morning as we walked through the capitol's spectacularly tiled vestibule, we spoke about what had just happened—how our mother had attempted to strangle me in my sleep. How freakish it seemed to stroll through that architectural marvel, blending in with all the tourists and summer vacationers as we wondered if our mother would try to kill us again.

STATE OF GRACE

❧

For the next few weeks, Lisa and I tossed and turned at night and woke from shallow slumber at the slightest noise. In our waking hours we tracked our mother's moods and expressions and hoped she'd soon find a job or become eligible for more public assistance. That, we thought, would be the key to her turnaround. She was out of cash now and couldn't buy cigarettes with food stamps. We were also into a second month of rent evasion and I didn't think the manager would let it slide any longer. Mom encouraged us to rehearse the lies we were to tell to the police, sheriff, or any public employee who might come to evict us. "Tell them he was fondling his penis. That's right, tell them Harry Brewster tried to molest you and that he was masturbating right there in front of you. Say it back to me, just like you would if I were a police officer." This from a woman who couldn't even tell me what a tampon was or how to use it!

"He was playing with his penis, and he was fondling me and masturbating," I repeated mechanically, not sure what it meant.

"No, simpleton!" she barked. "Say he was *fondling* his penis, *and* molesting you *and* masturbating in front of you. Say he had an erection, too! Now say it, simple. Say it until you get it right!" she commanded, becoming hysterical.

Pleasing my mother was not possible while she was in this state. I just hunkered down and hoped to avert a slap across the face or a shove through the doorway. I liked our apartment manager and thought, I don't want to say things like that about Harry. The worst thing he ever did was drink too much beer on the stoop and belch and laugh too loud sometimes.

My mother's rationale was that everyone would simply forget about evicting us if we introduced a distraction. Why couldn't we just say the faucet leaked or the toilet was always backing up? Wouldn't that give us some time? Couldn't we just go back to the welfare office and tell them there'd been no jobs, and we needed more food stamps and rent money? We began to recite more rosaries with our mother whenever we weren't practicing the molestation lie. Again we prayed for ten thousand dollars, but this time Lisa and I were wise enough to know it would never come.

Finally, one morning our mother asked us to sit with her at the table and listen to her plans. She told us that we were out of food, out of money, and out of time. We had been feeding our cat a mixture of beef organs and potatoes and whatever else we could find, since we had not been able to afford cat food for some time. We'd also been ripping up old sheets and stuffing them in our underwear for Kotex. She explained that what I had described some weeks earlier was a "prophetic dream" and that it foretold of a coming flood that would end the world as we knew it. She spoke at great length about the meaning of the various stories I had invented simply to quiet her. She said the crows were the apostles and that they were messengers from God. She told us that she, as "God's wife," would be required to do many things by His side to help Him make the transition from the world as we knew it to a new state of being, which would be a carefree, moneyless society—not quite earth and not quite heaven. She told us that there would be no pain, no injury, no poverty, no race, and no class in this new universe. She and God would be in charge. She assured us that this was all good news and that we needn't be anxious or afraid since she had been in constant communication with God about our course of action. Lisa and I sat wide-eyed and frightened as she gave us a specific date, which was approaching and by which we were to have left this earth to join God.

She then told us that we would be hanging ourselves as a family, from a pipe in the high ceiling of our apartment. In preparation, she said we were to return all of our library books and remove the perishables from the refrigerator to achieve the proper "state of grace." Then she told us to go outside and play while she spoke to God some more to get the particulars of her role. Lisa and I bolted from the house, terrified as we pondered our fate. What were we going to do now?

We talked about it all day and night. We thought that she might be right. She'd been saying she was God's wife and had a special purpose for as long as we'd known her, and had always told us that persecution was common for divine prophets. That made sense considering the things we'd been taught about the Messiah and the apostles from early on in Catholic school. Whenever we wondered aloud why *she* had been chosen, she jeered at us and explained that He would select only someone from a lowly station in life. "Of course He'd choose a black woman, simple," she'd curse. "Didn't you hear me tell you that 'the meek shall inherit the earth'? If you had been listening you'd know that, wouldn't you? Why do you think Jesus was born in a manger, Lauri? Because he was rich? You'd better hope you're in a state of grace when he sees you or else we'll be separated. I'll be going to heaven, and you . . . ?" She'd shrug.

"What if it's all true?" I asked Lisa. "She said if we don't go voluntarily before the flood comes, we too will be lost. I don't want to drown. At least if we hang ourselves *we'll* be doing it instead of waiting for the water to be over our heads."

"Yeah, and if Mom hangs herself and we don't and the flood doesn't come . . . well, I don't want to see that again," Lisa said.

We were torn because we did, in some sense, believe that a flood was on its way and that we'd be excluded from all the good times in the brave new world if we didn't swing with our mother. And besides, Mom was not giving us the option of staying here without her. "Does it take a long time before you black out?" I ventured timidly once.

"Don't be such an ass!" she retorted. "It doesn't hurt. . . . I've done it before and I should know!"

On the morning of July 28, 1972, Lisa and I lay in bed for some time, contemplating the reality of our last day on earth. We knew we would not defy our mother, and we also knew that it was unlikely that she would abandon her plan. While we were not ready to die, Lisa and I reviewed our lives and concluded that they had not been all that good anyway. Every sentence we spoke to each other began with, "Do you remember when . . ." and a melancholy pervaded our thoughts that morning as we remembered aloud everything from our mother's first committal and our stay at Cedar's to Mom's first hanging, to the Eaglestaffs, Uncle Itch, the Morrises, the Delgados, the Mbesis, St. Theresa's, St. Mary's, and everything that had happened up until then. I told Lisa I was sorry I had run away from her at Cedar's and that I wished I hadn't. I wanted her to know how much it had bothered me all those years. I also told her that I hoped our mother was right about the Hereafter, and she laughed a sad little laugh, saying, "Me too." And so my heart ached a little less as Mom walked into the living room from her bedroom.

"Are you girls ready?" she asked brightly, as if we were going to the movies.

"I guess so," we answered solemnly.

"Well, take this rope and string it over the curtain rod in the bath-room," she instructed.

The rope seemed much too short for its intended purpose, and we wondered why we were doing it in the bathroom instead of the living room as we had planned. Mom clarified, "This one is for Sugar Plum."

Lisa and I looked at each other, not quite able to understand what Mom was talking about. We had always assumed that Sugar Plum would stay in the apartment and be rescued by whoever discovered our bodies.

"You mean we're going to hang her, too?" I asked my mother.

Her answer came back in staccato blips: "What did you think, that we would leave her here to suffer?"

The thought of hanging our cat was too awful to comprehend. I felt physically sick at the prospect of carrying out this chore, as well as putting my own neck through a noose, but, dutifully, Lisa and I went into the tiny bathroom and hung the rope over the slender rod over the bathtub.

"I don't want to do this," I said to Lisa.

"Me neither," she answered, "but we've got to."

Our mother busied herself in the living room securing the ropes that would carry us to the other side. "Are you finished?" she called.

"Just about," I answered, stalling for a little more time.

"Good, then come in here and get the cat."

No nooooo nooooo, I thought. Don't make me do it, please, don't make me hang Sugar Plum. My eyes filled with tears as I dragged my feet into the living room and picked up the cat. I hugged her to my chest and whispered, "I love you, kitty" into her ear and asked her not to struggle. I told her I'd see her in heaven. I lifted her to the noose I'd tied, pushed her head through, and, despite her protests, withdrew my arms and let her drop. And then I ran. I ran from that bathroom as fast as I could and slammed the door behind me, completely distraught.

My mother shot me an icy look and asked, "Did you do it?"

"Yes," I said through my tears.

"Good. Now come here and help me get these chairs under the ropes."

Lisa and I were devastated by then; we couldn't look at each other. It had been a shitty life but we didn't want to die.

"Here," she said, "put that chair right under the rope." I did, then looked to her for further instruction. "Now, get up on it," she commanded. I obeyed, reluctantly. Lisa did the same. My mother then climbed onto her chair. We all stood, facing our nooses. Mom reminded us, "It will not hurt and there will be indescribable joy in a matter of seconds." I held on to this thought as I slipped the knotted rope over my head and prepared to step off the edge of the chair. Suddenly I caught something moving out of the corner of my eye. I turned to look and saw Sugar Plum, who must have slipped the noose, calmly strolling out into the living room. At first I thought that perhaps I *had* jumped and Sugar Plum was in heaven with us, but I quickly dismissed this notion.

"It's Sugar Plum. She got away," squealed Lisa in delight. We threw the ropes aside, jumped down and ran to embrace our beloved pet. "Sugar Plum, Sugar Plum, Sugar Plum," we could not stop saying her dear, sweet name. We looked at our mother, whose eyes had lost their steely resolve.

"Look, Mom, she's still alive!" I exclaimed.

Mom had to concede at this point that things did not look good for our suicide pact, at least not for that day. She sighed and told us to cut down the ropes while she asked God what to do next.

"Can we go outside?" I asked.

"Go ahead," she said, deflated.

And so it ended, a reprieve. For the want of a sturdy knot, the trajectory of our lives had once again been altered.

WORLD
WITHOUT END

❧

H is long wiry legs emerged from the back of a large purple car. He wore gold-rimmed sunglasses and had an Afro even larger than mine and the widest bell-bottoms I had ever seen. His strong jaws worked gum continuously into his perfectly white teeth as he smiled broadly at us. He leaped out and rushed to our side to open the car door to let us in.

"Ain't you a pretty little thing," he cooed. I felt my face warm as I returned his smile. "I'm yo' mama's *old-time* friend. Yeah, Wini and me go way back. My name's Chick Watts."

"Hi. Is this your car?" I ventured, shyly.

"This ain't no *car*, baby girl. This hyea's a Cadillac!" Chick winked.

I loved the way Chick walked and talked. There was a rhythm and cadence to him. He sort of glided for half a stride and, just at the last moment, danced a jaunty little hitch step that made his kinky black halo part, then whip right back into place. His creamy butterscotch skin invited touch.

Chick was the man who took us in when we were finally kicked out of the Orlo. I had been miserable to have to leave Sugar Plum with our old manager, Harry, but I knew that her life would be much better without us. Chick, I believe, had made my mother a deal. The deal might have been something like this: "Wini, you need a place to live, and I need some *female* companionship. Peaches, you *still* fine, your girls are well-behaved, and I still got all my own hair and teeth, what do you say?"

The deal was accepted, because before we knew it, we were in his purple Cadillac heading off to his house in the Malone District. Before she got into the car, Chick and Mom embraced briefly, and Lisa shot me a look as if they had just French kissed. We had hardly ever seen her hug anyone, let alone a man.

"Do you think they'll do it?" I asked Lisa later that night.

"I sure hope so," she said. "She could use it."

At that we'd both snickered into our pillows on the bed we shared at Chick's house. As we lay in the dark taking in all the new smells and sounds, Lisa and I tried to catch snippets of the conversation they were having in the kitchen: our mother's low murmurs, followed by staccato bursts of masculine laughter. Every few minutes we could hear the thunk of a bottle being set down on the kitchen table. We were also glad to hear that the conversation seemed to be going well. I was amazed at the inflections and tones my mother's voice began to take on out there. Her voice would rise occasionally to a level where Lisa and I could discern individual words and phrases, and they were unlike any we'd ever heard her utter before. "Ain't that a bitch, oooooh, honeychile." I heard her say the word "police," with the emphasis on the "po." We could hardly stifle our laughter as we lay there craning our ears. We heard Chick say tenderly, "You know, Peaches, it is so nice to jest be settin' here talking with you about all that mess we used to do when we was youngsters." Then there was a long pause. Lisa and I both forgot to breathe while we listened suspensefully for her reply. It came eventually, but not before Lisa and I guessed that they had been kissing.

"I'll be go to hell," Lisa said, "I think they're smooching."

"Me, too," I whispered with a mixture of delight and discomfort.

Mom murmured something softly to Chick.

All those years Lisa and I had fantasized about what Mom would be like with a man in her life, and here it was within earshot, and with a man we both liked. "I bet she'll be in a good mood tomorrow," I said to Lisa, as chairs scraped on the linoleum floor. "Shhhhh, they're moving into his bedroom!" I hissed to silence Lisa's giggles.

Just then our bedroom door opened and a beam of light shone in on me and Lisa as we slammed our eyes shut and tried to affect deep slumber. "Good night, Chick," my mother whispered. "Good night, Peaches," he called back sweetly. We heard Mom's footsteps as she tiptoed over to the double bed that Lisa and I shared. Gently, she nudged Lisa, who promptly faked a "sleep moan" and rolled over a little closer to me. I scooted to the edge, maintaining a constant deep breath that I hoped suggested stage-four sleep.

Mom eased into the bed beside us, and she herself began to breathe regularly as she drifted off. I thought my head might combust as I suppressed the irresistible urge to ask Lisa if she, too, could smell beer on Mom's breath. Our mother might be crazy, but she *never* drank. Oh, how I wanted to dish with Lisa at the latest developments in our lives. It was hard for me to get to sleep that night as I thought about how strangely our mother had behaved with Chick that night and how suddenly it had all ended. Part of me hoped, though, that the romance would continue to grow in the coming days.

Chick was a garbageman for the city of Lincoln and went to work before dawn each morning. Lisa and I came to love the sounds of his first waking moments. We'd hear him moving around in his room and then he'd make his way to the bathroom. We'd never heard pee sound so loud as it hit the bowl. It was as if someone was emptying a pitcher from a rooftop into a goldfish bowl, and it went on forever. Just when we thought he was done, a few more dribbles would drip out. Lisa and I took to betting how many splashes we would count before the flush.

Then began the shaving. Chick would slather a minty smelling cream on his face and rake the blade over every nook and cranny until he was smooth. Then he'd tap the razor on the edge of the sink and run it under hot water. That done, he'd shuffle into the kitchen in his robe and begin to make coffee. Minutes later we'd smell the coffee as it percolated on top of the stove. The aroma usually got my mother out of bed, and there Lisa and I would be without her, finally able to stretch out and gossip. They'd sit at his table and smoke for a little while and then he'd put on his jeans and coveralls. Mom would continue to talk to him through his bedroom door as he dressed. Her voice had become oddly more feminine in those days with Chick. Yet every night, Mom climbed into bed with us after a few beers with Chick, and before too long their relationship began to show the strain of his having a family to support. He probably figured he ought to be getting something more than companionship out of the deal, given that he was acting like a father and husband in many respects—paying the bills, keeping a roof over our heads, interacting with us kids—but getting less than he'd expected in return.

After a few weeks at Chick's, Mom began coming to bed without the beers, her voice sounding less girly and less ghetto all the time. They didn't outright argue, but I knew that he wanted his place back to himself. He still thought Lisa and I were cute; he cracked up one day when he came home from work to find us in two separate rooms with the big black telephone receivers to our ears, trading verses of the Jackson 5's "I'll Be There," singing harmonies with each other for the sheer thrill of using an extension line. "If that don't beat all," he chuckled. "I ain't never seen nobody get that much entertainment out of a phone." Chick should have been our dad, I thought. That would have been cool. I don't know what ultimately happened between them, but what I do know is that by the fall of that year, I found myself walking to Everett Junior High School from our new home at the Lincoln City Mission.

Homelessness as we now know it did not exist in Lincoln in 1972. There were no weary nomads with bundles of rags curled into storefront doorways, no plastic tarps suspended by hot air over exhaust grates, and no metal grocery carts piled high with junk propelled forward by their bedraggled owners. There weren't even any buskers pounding out Beatles songs on out-of-tune guitars for beer money. The only person I can remember who might qualify as a street person was an Indian woman whose greasy salt-and-pepper hair hung loosely from her drooping head where she sat every day on the corner of Thirteenth and O. Lisa and I named her Gotta Cigarette after the request she slurred to every passerby. She stationed herself along our school route, never failing to ask, even us, her favorite question. I always wondered where she went at night, and how she got money for food and clothes. I never actually saw her smoking, or, for that matter, doing anything but listing forty-five degrees against the JC Penney, repeating those same two words. As undesirable as our own situation had become, Lisa and I counted ourselves fortunate not to be quite as pathetic as Gotta Cigarette. If I had to be seen walking to my new school from the downtown City Mission past people who had real jobs and thriving careers, at least I didn't have to be filthy, smell like boozy vomit, and say the same thing all day.

Jodie Weitzman and I had not kept our promise to keep in touch over that summer. In fact, we hadn't spoken at all since the last day of grade school at Clare McPhee. I couldn't bear the thought of calling her from Chick's house to tell her we'd been evicted from the Orlo. Though we had become close, I never confided in her about the precariousness of my family life. I didn't want her to know that my mother was out of her mind, or that our apartment building was a ratty, falling-down wreck. I never invited her to visit my home.

She was a bit standoffish when we met for the first time in three months on that September day. "Did you guys go somewhere cool for summer vacation?" she asked tentatively.

"Naw, not really," I returned, evasively.

"Well, didja hang out with your old friends from St. Mary's or something?"

"Yeah, sometimes," I lied.

Finally, she asked, "How come you never called me?"

It killed me to have to act all nonchalant, as if I'd had better things to do than talk to my best friend. "I was just busy doing other stuff," I shrugged. Great, I thought, here I am on the first day of junior high and I can't even tell my only real friend that we were living in a downtown flophouse after shacking up with my mom's "boyfriend," after getting thrown out of the Orlo, where we hung ourselves *and* our cat. Oh, and did I leave out the part about Mom trying to strangle me after she stabbed the Dial Finance guy?

Unlike her family, we'd not gone to Six Flags over Texas or Lake of the Ozarks in our wood-paneled station wagon to splash in the sun and scream our brains out on thrill rides. Instead, we spent the summer hiding in the capitol, watching my mother's face for signs of trouble, concocting molestation accusations and reciting endless rosaries entreating the heavens to send money that never came. There didn't seem to be any good place to start explaining my real life, so I just lied or left things out.

Every day the lies got bigger. Luckily, Jodie Weitzman lived on Eleventh and C Street, directly across from Everett Junior High, so it was unlikely she'd ever walk me home. One afternoon, in sixth period, she came to me and announced that her mom was taking their beloved yappy Pomeranian, Skipper, to the vet and wouldn't be home until late. This was highly unusual, as Mrs. Weitzman hardly ever left the house. Because of this deviation in her mother's routine, she decided she would walk me all the way home to the Orlo, for the first time ever, that afternoon. Terror seized me, and I racked my brains for an excuse to make her go straight to her house after school and stay there. "My mom's on the rag this week, and she's being a real bitch," I explained, casually. "So you probably shouldn't even bother."

"Oh, who cares," she sang back. "Everybody's mom's a bitch. I'll just turn around when we get to your door."

"Jeez, Jodie, it's kind of far and it looks like it's gonna rain."

"That's okay," she returned, "I don't care if I get wet. I just wanna see what an apartment looks like. I've never been inside one." I had to think of a reason for her not to see where I lived.

The Orlo had been a castle compared to the cruddy four-story building in the industrial area of town that I now called home. Not only did Pastor Dunn and his wife, Eunice, look us up and down as if we were prostitutes when we walked in the front door, but we had to pass all these creepy-looking, unshaven men who leered at us as if they were planning a romantic evening for two in the alley later that night. We were the only females in the place other than Eunice, and we were consummately aware of that fact. Having explored every other possibility, Pastor Dunn had finally allowed us to stay at his Mission temporarily, since he didn't believe any of God's children should have to sleep outside.

In exchange for the privilege of eating in the Mission's dining room, we had to appear in the chapel promptly at six o'clock, primed for prayer, before we could experience the Lord's bounty. Missing the Sunday service was grounds for immediate dismissal.

The good reverend was hardly a nimble orator and those in attendance found it hard to remain upright while he droned, given their pounding hangovers and roiling guts.

I couldn't reveal this information to Jodie Weitzman as we trudged "home" with Lisa, who every so often would glare daggers at me.

I settled on a strategy of walking to the Orlo instead of the City Mission and stopping at the front of the entrance. I pleaded with my face and hands not to sweat or shake as I leaned against the stairs that went up to our old apartment. Oh God, please don't let our old neighbors or Harry Brewster come out and ask us what the hell we were doing back there and why the hell our mom hadn't come by with the big fat check she still owed for last summer.

Jodie chatted animatedly as she went on and on about the boys at school she thought were cute. I just wanted her gone. Every time a door opened or shut nearby, I feared that it would be someone who would recognize me. I couldn't even hear what she was saying anymore, so paralyzed was I by these thoughts.

"Don't you get it?" I wanted to explode. "I'm not like you. I don't have a house to go home to. My daddy doesn't work for Burlington Northern. We don't have a precious little fluffball named Skipper, and if we did we'd probably hang him! I'm never going to Six Flags over

Anything, and my mom's a fucking loonytoon!" My face remained impassive as my mind raced through this monologue. Suddenly, I noticed the silence as she waited for me to respond to some unheard question.

"Huh," I said vacantly.

"Jesus, what's wrong with you?" she snapped. "You're not even listening to me."

"Oh, well, I guess I'm thinking we better get going and help Mom with dinner or something, before she gets mad," I said, looking anxiously up into the window we used to rent.

"Jeez, are you uptight. Your mom must really be a bitch," she scoffed.

"Yup, she sure is," I agreed. "See ya!" I called back as my sister and I bounded up our old steps.

"Later," she replied dejectedly, turning to go.

We stood in the hallway for a few moments waiting for her to disappear. My sister looked down at the chipped and broken octagonal black-and-white tile underfoot. "That was close," she said. Then we walked out the front door, glancing to the right where Jodie had headed moments earlier, and slowly dragged our feet toward the Mission, where we hoped our mother would have some good news about a job or a real place to live.

HARD TIMES

❧

September stretched into October and crawled into November with still no word of employment or housing. During those months I enlarged my vocabulary to include words such as "delousing stations," "delirium tremens," "panhandling," "pedophilia," and "proselytizing." These were subjects my mother visited often when warning us girls what to look out for. She'd peel back her lips into a hideous curl and tell us, "You little girls had better watch out for that goddamn smelly-ass honky trash. If they're not trying to shove Jesus down your throat, they're trying to stick their dicks in you, get money from you, or infect you with their vile diseases. We'll be lucky if we get out of this godforsaken shithole without contracting TB."

Lisa and I took great pleasure in imitating Mom's facial contortions and bitter proclamations when she was out of earshot. As we worked our way through the dinner line at the Mission, I'd whisper to Lisa, "I'm gonna stab the next honky pigfucker that looks sideways at me, so help me God. You just wait and see if I don't splatter some pecker-wood's guts all over these walls tonight." Lisa would try not to spit her soup and to maintain some semblance of piety and gratitude in front of the Christian volunteers who fed us. I'd keep up this steady monologue with my mouth inches from her ear, right up to the point where I accepted my tray of slop. I'd barely finish saying the word "pigfucker," when the beneficent eyes of the missionaries would fall upon me as I humbly lowered my head and uttered a submissive "Thank you" to my server.

A lot of what Lisa and I said and did while we were at the Mission was not kind, but our banter helped us get through difficult times. My love for Lisa took the sting out of knowing we lacked so many of the things our friends and classmates had. I didn't know how much longer I could tell Jodie Weitzman "We're gonna get a phone next week" before she'd say, "Yeah right, and I'm gonna turn black." In our nightly conversations from the twin cots my sister and I slept in, we hoped aloud that we wouldn't have to spend the holidays at the Mission. Mom seemed to be going on some job interviews, and from what she told us, it also seemed that the pastor was helping her, even providing references, something she didn't really have since spending so much time in a mental institution.

In mid-November 1972, Mom met us with good news as we ducked and dodged our way home from school. We'd just walked into the door when she said breathlessly, "Good news, little dollies. I got a teaching job today!" All three of us jumped up and down and hugged and kissed as we chanted, "We got a job, we got a job, we got a job." My mind raced with thoughts of a new home with our own rooms and canopy beds and a color TV and a phone and maybe even another little cat. No longer would I have to dash out from my sixth-period class, avoiding Jodie Weitzman as best I could after the bell rang to meet up with my sister to walk to the Mission. I might even start getting an allowance. But for now, surviving the next few weeks until my mother's first pay-check arrived became our primary goal.

THE EAGLE FLIES

❧

I couldn't wait until *we* would again be among the privileged class: wage earners. I yearned to see my mother slap down a crisp twenty at the grocery store. The difference between those who paid cash and those who depended on the kindness of strangers had become abundantly clear to me in those months at the Mission. It wasn't that these folks were bad or disingenuous in any way, but their very presence provoked my mother to rail endlessly about their ineptitude and misguided intentions. She thought they were beneath her in every way, that they lacked the intelligence and life experiences that she herself possessed. "How is some snot-nosed honky bitch fresh out of Vassar going to know a fuckin' thing about life?" she'd practically scream at us.

"That harpy has more degrees than I have underwear, and she can't even pronounce 'Pagliacci.'"

Thanksgiving at the Lincoln City Mission was the last hurdle we would have to leap before my mother began her job teaching disabled kids at the Lancaster Office of Mental Retardation. For us, accepting this one final meal from the Mission would provide a fitting end for the months of degradation and deprivation. When the day arrived, Lisa and I waited with gleeful anticipation not only for a decent meal, but for the chance to witness the shock and humiliation register on the faces of the newcomers on this road to destitution. We knew there would be a lot of unfamiliar faces that day as Thanksgiving drew even the proudest of the poor to seek charity. Until that day, I don't know if I'd ever understood what "misery loves company" meant. I was tired of going to school and always being the worst off. While I wished them no harm, I longed to be in a crowd where I could look around and know for certain I wasn't at the bottom of the heap. As the doors opened to greet our "guests," Lisa and I suppressed grins at the line of people that snaked around the corner and into the alley.

We were not disappointed when a disheveled black woman with half a dozen kids plopped themselves down beside us at the long table. Lisa and I judged the kids to be about nine months and ten minutes apart in age, the youngest to be about six months old. There was no man with them. The mother was a deep, dark, rich, almost blue-black, as were all of her children. My mother gazed superiorly over the top of her head, trying to discourage conversation. After all, we were employed now and would soon be leaving.

"How you doin'?" the woman said to my mom.

"Hello," my mother replied frostily.

The woman didn't seem to notice the chill as she tried to keep an eye on her brood. "Damn, this meat look dry, don't it?" she directed at Mom as she lifted the fork over her baby's head to her mouth.

My mother didn't answer, so Lisa and I did, nodding and saying, "Yes," agreeably.

"Trivia, I'll snatch you bald-headed if you don't leave him alone!" she thundered suddenly, startling us all. It seems that one of her girls, about five years old, was teasing her brother by stealing his food. Lisa and I looked helplessly at each other. Had we heard that right? Yes, it seemed the child's name was, actually, Trivia. We deduced that they must not know what the word meant.

My mother's face had not changed upon hearing this name. The woman still hoped to converse with her, though perhaps she had begun to wonder if Mom might not be deaf or blind. "Look like your man up and left you, too," she chuckled, trying to find some common ground. "But at least he ain't left you with six of these"—she lifted her baby slightly from her lap—"and *this*," she said, pointing to her dark and swollen eye.

"I'm Wanda," she offered, extending the same hand that had just checked her infant's diaper. "Mrs. Jones," Mom said curtly. God what a bitch, I thought. Wanda's just trying to be friendly and my mom's acting like the queen of Sheba. "Where's Mr. Jones then?" Wanda returned, a little offended by now. Lisa explained that our father had been killed in a car accident some years ago, and then began asking her questions about her children and herself. Normally my mother would not have allowed such impudence, but this was a special occasion and we were being given some slack.

"I wish my girls was your age," Wanda said jovially. "I ain't had a break since I don't know when. I cain't wait to get this last one off the titty." My mother now clenched her fork as if she wished to put her own eye out with it. "Lord have mercy, between that worthless man and these chilren, these titties ain't seen the light o' day since I was about your age," she said, nodding toward Lisa. We waited breathlessly for Wanda's next revelation.

"Does your eye hurt?" I asked innocently, hoping to get some dirt on that situation. "No, chile, it don't hurt a bit no mo'. They gave me somethin' takes all the pain away at the hospital. I be *flyin'* on that stuff." My mother glowered at me, saying nothing, hoping to encourage us all to do the same. "He jes' went too far this time, my Johnelle, I cain't have that mess roun' these children," she continued. "He ain't worked steady since I met him. He like to smoke that weed, dontcha know. I could probly do better jes' getting a place with a girlfrien' or somethin' and sharin' expenses. I don't know what we gon' do for Chrismas, I ain't got two nickels to rub together this year," she lamented.

"Neither do we," I offered, beginning to like Wanda and her stream of consciousness chatter. It seemed as if she might be working up to suggesting that she and my mother pool their resources and try to dig their way out together.

Mom was choking down the last of her instant potatoes and making movements to wrap this party up when the pastor stood at the front of the hall and began tapping his glass with a fork. "Good people," he began. "It is so wonderful to see you all here on this glorious day as we pause to celebrate all we have to be thankful for." It occurred to me that most of the people in that room had precious little to be thankful for, but I listened on. "Lest we forget who is ultimately responsible for all that we have, let us bow our heads in prayer and thank our Lord for the gifts He has bestowed upon us this day." Mom didn't even pretend to bow her head as she scanned the room for an escape route. Wanda was trying to quiet her unruly children as we gave thanks with all the other bums, for the gray meat and gelatinous canned cranberry sauce. I took that opportunity to reflect on how grateful I was that we'd soon have a little bit of scratch and would be moving out of this dive. I never saw Wanda or Trivia or the rest of her brood again after that, but I do still think of them from time to time.

MY LITTLE
NIGGERS

⁂

M om began work that Monday at LOMR, which we pronounced
"Lowmar." We told her that she looked beautiful as she applied
her lipstick and "picked out" her modest 'fro. Lisa and I stood behind
the mirror as Mom took extra time to adjust her collar and scan her face
for blemishes. She raised her head as she often did to check the dark
crosshatched rope burn just under her chin. It was becoming less visi-
ble with each passing year. Our job was to prevent even the slightest
kernel of doubt to creep into her psyche as she prepared for the day
that lay ahead.

All three of us left the Mission together and walked toward our re-
spective schools. Lisa and I parted ways with Mom after three quarters of

a mile as she headed east and we went west. "We love you, Mom," we called after her as she turned to go. Looking back momentarily she responded in kind, "I love my little niggers, too." That felt sweet, since she only called us "my little niggers" when she was in an affectionate mood. We hoped for the best as we headed to Everett.

T wo weeks later, Mom had her first paycheck in hand. She didn't have a bank account so she had to go to Klein's Grocery to cash it. Things were different back then. Local businesses tried to help you out every now and then. If you lived in the neighborhood, you didn't have to show a driver's license or give up 10 percent of the check. They'd just look at you, ask if the check was good, make a judgment call, and hand over the cash. Mom signed the check over to Wes Klein, and he opened the register and gave her the cash. Real green money, which we hadn't seen in some time. He counted it out to her with respect and dignity and made no mention of the fact that he knew we'd always used food stamps before. Mr. Klein never held against her the many tongue lashings she had delivered him for myriad perceived slights. I remembered standing before him in agony as she launched into a tirade about the inconvenience he'd caused her by insisting she send a note giving us permission to buy cigarettes for her. "How dare you insinuate my girls are buying the cigarettes for themselves. My daughters are sterling," she seethed.

"Yes'm, I know the girls don't smoke," he'd say, politely, "but I need to have that note in the cash register in case the state checks up on me someday. You know it is against the law to sell them to minors, but since I know you and the girls, I try to make it easy on you. But I do need that note, Miz Jones." I thought Mr. Klein was a nice man, and I wanted to slap my mother for being so hostile.

1210 F STREET

E d *and Vesta Voight* stood at the doorway of their first-floor apartment gripping the application clipboards and listening to my mother speak. They were in their sixties and both had cigarettes dangling from their mouths as they watched us. When it was their turn to speak, ashes shook loose at will from the ends of their "cherries" and onto the green shag carpet beneath them. My mother never smoked without having her hands poised elegantly before her in the two-finger hold that I thought separated class from trash. Vesta looked like an old party girl who'd finally had enough and settled down here to spend her last days living in and managing these apartment units. Even when we met her at this advanced age, she wore her slacks so tight they nearly cleft her in two. "Smuggling yo-yos" is what we called it. I later learned that she'd been named after the vestal virgins of Roman mythology. By the time I learned that, I also knew that her name was probably the only virginal thing about her.

The apartments were relatively new, clean, and tidy. "How old are you?" Ed aimed at me. "Twe—" I started to answer before being cut off by my mother, who spat, "Thirteen, and Lisa is fourteen." "Well, we don't usually have no kids in here," said Vesta from behind Ed in her low, smoke-damaged voice. "A lot of the folks who live here are older and retired and they don't like a lotta noise, you see," she continued. What she didn't say was that they were also all white.

"My girls are extremely quiet and studious," assured my mother, "and would never be a problem." Lisa and I smiled sweetly to emphasize her point. Mom kept me to the fore, partially obscuring Lisa, whose skin tone could have been a deal-breaker. We understood we were to say nothing at all for the rest of the conversation. My youth was a far lesser offense than Lisa's darkness. "I work near here and the girls attend school close by. It's an ideal location for us and we'd love to move in immediately if we could," Mom pressed, despite the anxious looks on the Voights' faces.

"The vacant unit is directly over us and we'll know right away if there's any monkey business going on up there. That's why we want to be extra careful with who we get in there," explained Ed, trying to scare us off. What he didn't know was that we'd just spent the last few weeks with a bunch of consumptive, louse-ridden, alcoholic pedophiles, and we didn't scare easily.

"Since my husband's death, I've had no interest in anything but raising my girls and teaching school," Mom said wistfully. This got the attention of Vesta, who looked at her own dear Ed and tried to imagine a life without him. The pining widow ruse always worked, I thought as I watched Vesta's face shift from suspicion to pity. I let my own face droop and willed my lip to quiver as I remembered my dear father taken from us so prematurely, so cruelly.

"Oh, goodness, dearie, how did it happen?" queried Vesta.

"He died in a car accident," answered Mom. I could tell Vesta thought the misfortune had occurred in the recent past and my mother did nothing to set her straight. "You must have had a hard go of it then, ever since," surmised Vesta. By this time I knew we had them. "Do you have any references, honey?" asked Vesta, almost apologetically.

"Well, we don't have many; my husband used to handle everything, but perhaps the reverend from our church could write something," half-truthed Mom.

"Oh yes, dear, that would be lovely," ventured Ed grandfatherly.

We returned the same day and placed the letter of referral from Pastor Dunn into Ed's warm hands as we prepared to begin our new lives in the furnished one-bedroom apartment above the Voights'.

Three black plastic bags and a couple of cardboard boxes were all we had to move into the new apartment. It must have looked mighty sorry to the Voights, who stood in the courtyard as Pastor Dunn pulled up in his station wagon and helped us carry things inside.

Generic beige carpet, a picture window that looked out onto the alley, a psychedelic paisley couch, one yellow beanbag chair, a tiny kitchenette with a pink half-fridge stashed under the countertop, a two-seat dinette with a fold-out leaf, one medium-sized chest of drawers, and a double bed in the only bedroom. That's what we got for our $145 a month at 1210 F Street and boy, did it seem like a lot.

Lisa and I were thrilled with our new riches. "Look, Lisa," I squealed, "you swivel this one handle and the water goes from hot to cold!"

"Dang!" she returned, awestruck.

"A view!" I shouted, almost pulling the drapes from the wall as I ripped them open. I looked out onto the Dumpsters in the alley and the back wall of the apartment building opposite ours. "Dibs on the couch," I hollered gleefully, proud that I'd thought to claim my sleeping preference before Lisa.

She pouted. "Well, where am I going to sleep?"

Mom slammed her palm on the top of the dresser. "Oh for God's sake, we haven't even put our shit down, and you evil monsters are fighting. Why the hell do I even bother trying? I might as well just lay down and die."

Silence fell over us and I was sorry I'd ruined the moment. "We can take turns," I offered weakly, glancing toward Lisa with my head down. Lisa and I began quietly taking what few things we had out of the bags and boxes and putting them where we thought made sense. Mom did the same in what was without question *her* bedroom. Since there was only one chest of drawers and one closet in the entire apartment, Mom said we could share them with her and retrieve our clothes from her room each morning as we dressed for school. We divvied up drawers and shelves, and the atmosphere began to lighten up as the excitement over our new digs gradually began to take hold.

Klein's store, only a block away, was now closer and more convenient than ever. We were hungry, but Lisa and I kept our mouths shut, not wanting to irritate Mom with dinner requests or suggestions. We assumed we'd be sent to Klein's for a few groceries and hoped that a frozen pizza would be among them. All three of us had noticed the huge neon horse suspended over Bronco's, the fast-food joint on Thirteenth Street, as we'd driven in with the pastor, but Lisa and I hadn't even dared hope for that. But Mom said, "How would you girls like to take this five-dollar bill and get us some burgers down the street?"

Oh pinch me! I thought. "Let's go, Lise!" I said, not bothering to grab a jacket as we snatched the bill from our mother's hand and ran.

We returned home about twenty minutes later with a feast. To this day, I don't believe anything has ever tasted so good in my life as did that first meal at 1210 F.

That night I slept on the hard, short couch, springs poking my sides and hip bones and one of the matching sofa pillows under my head. Lisa slept on the floor beside me, the two cushions of the couch shoved together beneath her. With a sheet and a blanket with the words "City Mission" stamped in blue dye in the corner covering us, we fell asleep and dreamed about the next day.

ANTICIPATION

✺

Standing backstage at our school auditorium waiting to go on, I was terrified. What had possessed me to want to sing in the Christmas program? I didn't know if I could pull this off and dared not imagine what life would be like at Everett Junior High if I were to forget the words or lose my place on the fret board. My hands sweated and I paced nervously as I waited for the eighth-graders to wrap things up onstage.

At the last minute, the Desmond twins had been added to the bill as a consolation prize for their second-place finish in the talent contest that had been conducted to decide who would fill the "featured guest" slot on the Christmas program that year. Though I had been, to my surprise, chosen the winner of the contest, theirs had been a much more traditional choice of music, which satisfied the administration's preference for holiday fare. Our reward was to present our award-winning performances for the entire student body and their parents. Usually, there were no individual performances, other than a brief solo within a choral arrangement, but this year was different because Everett Junior High School had a new music teacher, Anna Shoemaker, who was eager to make her mark in her new environment.

Midyear, Mrs. Shoemaker replaced Mrs. Timms, whose fragile con-stitution had not lent itself to teaching public school teenagers. Mrs. Timms had taken to ingesting prescription medications in an effort to calm her frayed nerves, made increasingly so by the high jinks of the spirited youths in her charge. Worn raw by the constant chatter, defi-ance, and gum-cracking of her students, she found solace, at least ini-tially, in the euphoria produced by whatever it was she took each morning.

Lisa noticed first that her thin, pale, nearly translucent skin had be-come even more transparent of late, as her blue veins seemed to draw a road map to her vital organs. Mrs. Timms had always seemed frail to me, and she appeared to be a goody-goody Christian-type lady with her lilt-ing Southern accent. The thought of her being "high" enthralled me. "I'm going to check her out really close tomorrow in glee class," I promised Lisa, hoping to see further signs of decline. I hadn't been alone in my "stoner watch." At lunch, everyone was talking about what had "come over" Mrs. Timms. "Maybe she's pregnant," someone speculated as the rumor mill ground at full capacity. "Maybe she's drunk," chimed in an-other, quickly followed by a delirious, "Maybe she's mainlining heroin!"

In class that day, Mrs. Timms, halfway through a song she was teaching us, slumped forward over the keys of the piano and raised a willowy hand, asking for assistance into the teacher's lounge. Becky Perkins rose to help her. The rest of us sat frozen in our chairs. She gently guided Mrs. Timms, who swayed to and fro on shaky legs. Once standing, she suddenly clapped her cupped palm to her mouth as she tried to suppress her sudden need to vomit. Becky tried to distance herself from the emesis as they struggled toward the door.

The next day, a substitute teacher, Anna Shoemaker, arrived. We all hoped to quickly discover her weaknesses and prey upon them. We were told that Mrs. Timms would be on leave for an indefinite period of time, but she did plan to return when "she felt a little better." A week turned into two weeks, which turned into a month, and before we knew it, Mrs. Shoemaker was the full-time replacement for Mrs. Timms as our glee teacher. Anxious to present herself as energetic and motivated, Mrs. Shoemaker took on the school's annual winter concert as her first big production. She wanted the show to be a knockout and decided that a talent showcase during the regular program might be the perfect addition.

That's how I found myself peering through the curtains backstage, waiting for the chubby, freckled Desmond twins, Sandra and Saundra, to conclude their rendition of "Little Drummer Boy." I had never been popular or recognized as a musical talent in any of the schools I'd attended, and I was determined to distinguish myself in the eyes of my classmates this year. Having attained some measure of comfort, and past the point of being reviled, as in Catholic school in Omaha, I was no longer content with just "getting by" in school. I wanted to be known for doing something better than average. Ultimately, I wanted to be cool, and so I'd auditioned for and won a spot in the concert. But at that moment, as I gazed at the pimply, red-haired Desmond girls in what seemed to be the fifty-second verse of the song, I felt anything but cool. I felt doomed.

Things were not going well for the twins. Their instructions had been to step forward from the risers as their eighth-grade glee class finished their last song. Poor planning had positioned them on the top level and they had to push awkwardly past their classmates, picking their way painstakingly down each tier in their platform shoes. After starting the song promisingly, their pitches began to wander. They did not seem to notice that the piano remained in the same key, while they had descended nearly a half step by only the second round of "pah rump a pum pums." By the third verse they'd slid nearly a whole note south of where they should have been.

Sensing something was wrong, but unable to correct it, they darted nervous looks at each other as they continued to sing. Their voices became thin, reedy, and almost inaudible as their confidence drained away. Mothers began plastering gentle, understanding looks on their faces as they stared at the stage, trying to project calm as we all witnessed the girls' panic. Fathers' eyes threw silent daggers at their younger children who snickered openly while watching the nightmare unfold. No longer able to think clearly, both of the pale, plump girls had begun to forget the words. One sang, "the ox and lamb kept time" at the same moment the other intoned, "our newborn king to see." At least they got out there without tripping, I thought, trying to glean some good from the carnage unfolding before my eyes. As I watched them glare unspoken accusations at each other, I tried to telepathically convey the words "abort, abort, abort," as I felt an unexpected surge of compassion for them. To orient the girls, the accompanist, Jane Herriot, had begun humming loudly and feeding them the lyrics, all to no avail. Parents had lost control of their children by this time. Some were laughing aloud.

Sandra, having had enough, turned tail and ran off the stage, leaving her twin, Saundra, to fend for herself. Mrs. Shoemaker finally strode quickly onto the stage, grandly announcing, "The Desmond Sisters! Let's give them a big round of applause, folks!" An eternity later a smattering of mercy clapping dotted the auditorium as parents murmured that the new teacher should not have allowed things to go on so long before intervening.

After the twins' humiliating performance, I abandoned all thoughts of "cool" and hoped only to make it through the performance from start to finish. In a silent prayer I thanked God that my own mother was not there, as she religiously eschewed school social functions. I wondered if we might not just call the whole program off at this point. Let's just get our coats on, go home, and cut our losses, I thought desperately. Frantic, I looked to the risers, trying to pick out Jodie Weitzman's face among those of my classmates. No comfort could be found there as I realized that those in the choir had a sense of superiority born of the relief that it would be me, and not them, walking out alone in front of the still tittering crowd, after the Desmond debacle. I heard my name announced and made a wide berth around the sobbing Desmond girls as I came onto the stage with my borrowed guitar. Mrs. Shoemaker stood beside me for an instant quieting the audience before bolting backstage to prepare the choir for the rest of the show.

"Just hit the D and don't fuck it up," I told myself as I commanded my fingers to form the chords I had memorized from the songbook my mother had bought me. The fret board of my guitar looked as if it had dropped into my hands from outer space, and I could not remember what the dots meant. I'd rehearsed the song at least a hundred times in our apartment while looking out the picture window into the alley, but hell if I knew what to do at that moment. How could a few hundred people be so quiet? Why were they all staring at me? I could still hear the Desmond twins snuffling backstage as Mrs. Shoemaker murmured soothing words to them. Now what? As if Gepetto were pulling my strings, my fingers began to form themselves commandingly around the neck of the guitar. I strummed the D chord powerfully and slid my pinkie up a half step to get the little grace note I loved so much. My eyes became fixed on the crowd in front of me as if I truly believed I had something valuable to say, something they could not miss. I paused to let the D resonate and to lure people into wondering if I'd lost my will. Then I began with, "We can never know about the days to come. But we think about them anyway." My voice rang out clearly, my guitar sounded crisp and distinct, and I became aware that I had the full attention of every person in that auditorium.

Things had gone well so far, but I still had to get to the first chorus. I hurtled toward the B section of the song. Here we go. "An-ti-cipation. Anticipation is making me late . . . Is keeping me waiting." Okay, that felt good. There's no denying that chorus felt real good. Now let's hit the second verse before I get cocky. Before I knew it, I was singing the last words of the song: "So stay right here, 'cause these are the good ol' days, these are the good ol' days." I hit the high note at the end, and a gasp whooshed past my ears. I wasn't sure what it was, but I finished the phrase anyway, and to my astonishment the whole auditorium leaped to its feet and began a thunderous clapping and hooting that shook the rafters. Children and parents alike stomped the floor and whistled as if it were a pro wrestling match. I stood in disbelief as the house came down. There in the Everett Junior High School auditorium, soaking up all that positive energy, I understood that I would never do anything else for the rest of my life but sing.

THE SHADE

ॐ

After my performance I must have walked backstage and rejoined my seventh-grade glee class, but if so I don't remember. I must have seen Jodie Weitzman and my other classmates, but I don't remember that either. I must have gotten on those risers with everyone else and sung the songs we'd prepared as a group, but that too is gone. What I do remember is going to school the next day and having people I didn't even know clap me on the back and say, "Hey, nice job last night" or "You really nailed that song." I beamed everywhere I went. Teachers whose classes I wasn't in winked at me. Parents congratulated Mrs. Shoemaker on a good show. "Hey Laura!" kids yelled from halfway down the hall. I'd look up and they'd sing "Anticipation," strumming air guitar. I loved that. Kids started calling me "Bush" because of my big Afro. I loved that, too. It seemed those three minutes reversed the direction of my life. Those three minutes paved the way for the happiest three years of school I would ever experience.

Singing that song gave me the confidence to become involved with other school activities. I became an A student in nearly all of my classes. By the eighth grade, I was completely immersed in gymnastics and competitive trampoline. The federal government had recently instituted Title IX, which mandated that girls and boys were to have equal access to education and physical fitness programs. That year, I became all-city trampoline champion. Olga Korbut and Nadia Comaneci became my heroes. My mom, seeing my enthusiasm, even enrolled me in a gymnastics school run by the University of Nebraska head coach, Francis Allen. Our coach, Carolyn Benfeldt (or Bennie as we lovingly called her), began taking me to gymnastics clinics to expose me further to the sport, sometimes at her own expense.

Things were going great and I could feel the anger subsiding in me with each passing day. Rochelle and Marilyn Monroe were but distant memories. Our mom's attempted suicide and our year at Cedar's seemed surreal. The bad times, though fairly recent, no longer had the power to haunt me, or to make me hurtful toward others. By the time I graduated from junior high in 1975, I had not missed a single day of school in three years. To my surprise, I was given the only award in my graduating class for perfect attendance, a reward I never would have thought possible three years earlier.

All through my years at Everett my mother attended work regularly, and though still not stable or socially at ease, she loved many of the children she taught at LOMR. She spoke almost nightly with deep affection of a little boy named Roger who'd fallen down the stairs in his walker as an infant and been permanently brain-damaged. There was also Sandy, who was autistic and whose gentle mischief my mother found irresistibly charming and precious. Mom took pleasure that LOMR did not attract many "normal" people to teach its special-needs children. Many graduates fresh out of UNL Teacher's College found themselves ill at ease when presented with the physical appearance and alarming sounds of some of these kids. Many chose instead to instruct the "less challenging" children enrolled in public school.

My mom's colleagues tended to be a bit idiosyncratic. There was Paul, the homosexual transvestite, who taught along with his lesbian wife, Annie. Others were downright nuts. Though my mother may have been the nuttiest of all, she had an immense gift for reaching those kids. Parents would stop my mother on the street and embrace her, gushing praise for the remarkable progress they'd seen in their children. Mom believed deeply in the rights of these children to have dignity, love, and acceptance as well as access to the best education their individual learning capacities allowed. Roger was thirteen years old and his entire vocabulary consisted of three words. One of those words was "Wini."

DO YOU LIKE
TO SEW?

❧

I got *friendly that year,* 1973, with a boy named Eldon Min-
nieweather, who outright adored me. He looked a little bit like a
teenage Michael Jackson, ran track, and knew karate. I, too, partici-
pated in track and field, and we clandestinely eyed each other as we
practiced our individual events after school. I nearly swooned when
he'd run up to me in his little white gym shorts and put his arm around
me. As cute as I found him, his grades were atrocious, and I took it
upon myself to tutor him. Before and after school we'd take walks and
find quiet places to make out. I still remember his beautiful white teeth
as he grinned down at me and invited, "C'mon baby, let's get it on." On
weekends we'd walk to the capitol and find a corner where we could

grind on each other for hours. Eldon's promising older sister, Phyllis, was sixteen, unwed, and pregnant. Phyllis's loss of options distressed his family, and his mother lectured him daily about the dangers of fornication before wedlock. These admonitions were always at the fore as we groped our way through those years doing everything but "the deed."

Things were looking up that eighth-grade year. I had a boyfriend, I was popular, I liked my teachers, and I was getting good grades. Bad news was becoming a relatively rare event until, toward the end of that year, Mrs. Benfeldt called me into her office and asked me if "I liked to sew." I could think of few pastimes I liked less. I wasn't fond of most feminine pursuits and had been elated when Lincoln public schools loosened its gender-based class requirements that year, which allowed me to avoid home economics and opt for wood shop instead. Eldon, on the other hand, was thrilled to be one of the first males in home ec. He thought it would be great to learn to cook and sew and couldn't wait to impress me with what he'd baked. Given my disdain for domestic chores, it came as a shock when Bennie popped the sewing question. Out of practice with lying, I responded, "God, I'd rather die!"

Her face fell as she sat before me at her desk and pulled something from beneath it. I looked at it, perplexed. "It's a sewing box," Bennie said as I gazed down at the ornate square blue woven basket with a delicate cedar handle. "I've had it for some time, and now I want you to have it—as a going-away present. I'm leaving Everett." Embarrassment and grief hit me in equal measure as I tried to process what she'd said.

"Wh-what do you mean?" I stammered.

"My husband, Jim, is graduating from the university in a few weeks and we are going to move to Gibbon and farm. We also want to start a family."

"Why do *you* have to go, too?" I almost cried. "Couldn't he just start the farm without you and you stay here for a few more years?"

Bennie took my hand gently and said, "Things just don't work like that. You'll understand better when you get married and start your own family." I cried right there in her office and tried to hide my face in my hands. I hated crying in front of people, but I just couldn't help it. Bennie had done so much for me, and I wanted so badly for her to stay. "You'll have a great gym teacher next year, Laura," she said to me. "I know her. Her name's Mrs. French, and you'll probably like her even better than me."

"No I won't. I just know I won't," I disagreed, inconsolable as I left her office clutching the now-precious sewing basket in my hand.

A few weeks after the school year ended, Bennie threw a going-away party in her tiny apartment for all her favorite students. My heart felt so heavy I could hardly enjoy myself. Jodie and I stayed after everyone had left, and I told Bennie I would write her often. She promised the same and we all hugged and said our good-byes.

Summer crept by. I dreaded being at home all day. I hated waking up, hearing Mom get ready to go to work, knowing that I did not have school to attend. More time at home meant more time to worry about my mother's state of mind. Some days she'd come home to cheerfully regale us with stories of her day. "Guess what Sandy did today?" she'd laugh. We'd listen enthusiastically for the story. Other days she was more likely to say something like "That Jew bitch Rachel Goldberg thinks she knows everything. How dare she call me to the carpet. I know which 'focus tools' Danny needs to be 'on task.' I know what's effective with Sandy. That little chippy doesn't know shit. She's just jealous because I'm better than she is with those kids."

At those times even Paul and Annie, who she worshipped for their odd take on life and strange marriage arrangement, were not immune to her barbs. "Those motherfucking freaks probably smoke dope and have sex with those snakes they keep in their apartment. God only knows what kind of sick-ass shit they do behind closed doors. Who in the hell would want a boa constrictor for a pet anyway, besides some sick-ass freak?" On those days I would look at the calendar and count the hours until school began again. On those days, 1210 F Street seemed like a prison.

UNDERSTANDING
FRENCH

❧

The summer eventually passed and just after Labor Day, 1974, I began my last year at Everett Junior High. My first-period class went smoothly, as did the second. Then came the one I'd been dreading, third-period gym class. How could I walk into that gym that held so many dear memories and not see Bennie? I didn't even want to look at the trampoline, or the balance beam, or any apparatus for that matter, if Bennie wouldn't be showing me what to do with them.

I walked into the gym past a smiling brown-haired woman holding a clipboard and a whistle. I did not return the smile as she asked my name. "Laura," I answered dully, not meeting her gaze.

"Do you have a last name?" she chirped gaily.

"Yeah," I grunted as I shouldered past her and sat on the gym floor with the other ninth-grade girls. Those of us who'd been particularly fond of Bennie sat in silence, staring poker-faced at our Peachee folders.

"Hi, everybody. My name's Mrs. French, and I'm going to be your gym teacher and coach this year. Now I know as ninth graders you're probably used to doing things a certain way, so I hope you'll bear with me as I learn the ropes here at Everett. I don't have a lot of rules, but I do need for everyone to be on time, listen to me, and respect one another during my class." I let out a disdainful snort as I looked around at the others and rolled my eyes. "I'll need to take roll, get your birth dates, and check your schedules before we go any further."

I yawned loudly as she began to read her enrollment list. Mrs. French looked up briefly and then went back to her list. Kim Rodriguez sat on the floor next to me and I leaned over to her. "Check this out," I said as I began answering "Here" to every name being read. Unable to identify the source, Mrs. French asked that we please not answer until our names had been called. She went back to reading the names from her clipboard. "Pauline Christiansen," she called.

"Here," I answered simultaneously with Pauline.

The whole room began to snicker. Mrs. French, irritated by this time, put down her clipboard and asked who had been answering out of turn. I looked around innocently with the other girls as I tried to convey my eagerness to catch the culprit. Many of my classmates began to talk among themselves as respect for Mrs. French began to diminish. Then she dropped her pen and I laughed and taunted, "Are you a spaz?" Many in the room began to laugh with me as we unraveled her.

"Is there a particular reason you're behaving this way?" Mrs. French then asked me pointedly.

"Is there a particular reason you're behaving this way?" I mimicked cruelly to the hoots and hollers of my fellow classmates. Finally, no longer

able to control the class or hide her hurt, Mrs. French turned on her heel and walked briskly from the gym and into her office.

Kim and I sat on the floor and stared at each other, stunned that my ploy had been so effective. Silence enveloped the class as we sat there, the clock ticking. I wondered what she was doing in there. "Do you think she's calling the principal?" I asked Kim weakly.

"I don't know," she shrugged.

"Why isn't she coming out?" I continued.

"Beats me," said Kim. The other girls in my class began to look awkwardly at each other and then at me and my face began to burn as they took me to task.

"Smooth move, Ex-Lax. Why'd you hafta do that?"

"Well, I guess I didn't think she'd take it that hard," I defended lamely.

"Now what're you gonna do?" asked someone else, placing the blame for this whole situation squarely on my shoulders.

"How the hell should I know!" I shot back.

"Well, you sure knew everything five minutes ago," quipped another.

I gazed at the clock and noticed there were twenty minutes remaining in that period. I glanced sheepishly at Kim and said, "You wanna come with me and see what she's doing?"

"Ummm," she replied hesitantly.

"C'mon, I can't just march in there by myself," I pleaded.

"Oh, okay," she complied.

I got up quickly, extending my hand to help her from the floor before she changed her mind. All eyes were on us as we stepped lightly across the varnished wooden floor and into the office.

Timidly, I opened the door a crack, glad that it hadn't been locked. As I pushed it open, I saw Mrs. French sitting at her desk, with her chair turned in the opposite direction, facing the bookshelves on the wall. Her feet were propped up on the shelves as she leaned back and surveyed the instructional manuals before her. I thought she might say something but she didn't.

The silence unbearable, I finally spoke. "I guess you're probably wishing you weren't here with us," I ventured.

A sad, quiet, "huh," came from her as she continued to look at the bookshelves before her. I noticed that she'd been crying. Kim stood silently beside me. Seeing the hurriedly dried tears on Mrs. French's face softened me instantly and made me feel like a jerk.

"Look, I'm sorry I acted like that out there. I just got carried away. We really loved Bennie—she taught us last year. I guess that's why I was being so mean. I guess that really wasn't too cool, huh?"

"Well, no, I guess it wasn't," replied Mrs. French, to my relief. I was glad to see she could still talk. "Carolyn and I were in a lot of classes to-gether at the U," she continued. "I liked her, too. It's just that it's my first year teaching full-time and I hoped it would start out better than this."

"Oh boy, that's for sure!" I heartily agreed. "Hey look, me and Kim used to help Bennie take roll sometimes and maybe we could do that for you, too, if you want. I mean, since we know pretty much everyone from last year and everything."

"That would be helpful," said Mrs. French, softly.

"You want us to do it today?" I asked hopefully.

"Sure," she said quietly, and with that the three of us walked out into the gym and took roll.

By winter of that year, Mrs. French had become "Frenchie" to me, and from that day forward, we never had problems. Indeed, that day was the start of a continuing friendship I still have, some twenty-seven years later, with Kathy French. Though I think she preferred coaching team sports over gymnastics, she hung in there with me through the season, which culminated in the perfection of a maneuver on the uneven parallel bars that I'd been working on for over a year. The move is called an Eagle, and by today's standards, the stunt is rudimentary, but at that time, it had been mastered by only a few ninth-graders in the Lincoln public school system. For days Frenchie stood by the uneven parallel bars, evaluating my form and encouraging me to try again.

The skill involves a kip mount onto the lower bar, progressing to a wraparound, and ending in a reverse grip backward explosion onto the high bar. It was a "blind" trick in that you could not see where you were going to end up as you flew through the air. You have to intuit where the bar is behind you. I'd practice the sequence often forty times after school, only to find myself too early, too late, or too forceful to grab the upper bar. I hoped to master the elusive Eagle before the all-city gymnastics meet, which took place at the end of the season. I just couldn't seem to accomplish the maneuver with any reliability. How patient and giving Frenchie had been as she stood there, sometimes an hour or longer after everyone else had left, shouting instructions and encouragement to me.

The big day arrived, and I found myself standing before the city judges as I smiled and waited for the signal to begin. I'd been chosen to compete for Everett in the all-around category, which meant that I would be required to do a routine on each apparatus. I'd already competed and won first place on the trampoline. Of the remaining events (floor exercise, balance beam, vaulting horse, and uneven parallel bars), I had done well on the floor exercise. In order to medal in the all-around one had to finish in the top three in the cumulative scoring. I was still in the running as I stood before the uneven bars. Mrs. French stood beside me, spotting and ready to catch me if I fell, which was likely, judging from my low success rate in practice. I wore a long-sleeved, tie-dyed leotard to hide the rows of bruises on my forearms bearing witness to my many failures.

I began my mount by jumping up, hands extended before me in

preparation to kip to the lower bar. I continued on with the series of required elements. I swung smoothly from the high bar and wrapped my torso around the low bar. So far the routine had gone without a hitch. As I completed my wrap, I gathered myself to reverse my grip, propel myself backward, and catch the high bar. I felt cool air rushing through my Afro and hitting my scalp as I popped off the lower bar, arms extended behind me. To my amazement, I found myself hanging, perfectly whole, hands turned backward, from the high bar, just as if I'd planned it. My mouth flew open in a spontaneous burst of joy as I stuck that Eagle. I shot a glance to Frenchie, who beamed back at me. As soon as I completed my dismount she rushed into view and began crying and hugging me and shouting, "You did it! You stuck it! Thatta girl. You did it!" over and over again.

Even with the successful completion of that Eagle, I failed to place in the top three, but I could not have cared less. Frenchie had hung in there with me through the whole season, even after I had made her cry on that first day of school. All of that struggle and all of those failures and all of that hard work came together for the two of us at that moment when my hands grasped the bar and held me there those few seconds, and as far as I was concerned, I could have finished dead last and it would not have mattered. I have had only a few moments as pure and perfect as that in all of my years.

THE WINTER
OF '75

∝

While *tension mounted* at home the better part of my ninth-grade year, I tried to ignore it and take refuge at school. Mom resented my attachment to my teachers, past and present. One December day, Bennie and her husband came to Lincoln to get supplies and have a weekend off the farm. They dropped by our apartment unannounced to see if I wanted to accompany them to a University of Nebraska football game, as they had an extra ticket. I'd never been to a live football game and I pleaded with my mother to let me go. "No, I'm sorry, we need Lauri here at home today," she said coolly.

Incensed, I remained silent and sullen for the rest of the day as I stewed about my mother's refusal. There'd been nothing of particular importance on our plate that day and I wasn't at all critical to any project she'd planned. Noticing my bitterness at dinner she tossed her head at me in contempt. "You'd see how much that honky bitch cared for you if she had to put up with your simple ass day in and day out like I do. I bet she wouldn't find you so cute then." I wanted to leap from the table and rip her throat out, but instead I lowered my eyes and continued to eat in silence.

Most of my friends' parents would have been thrilled to have an honor student who came home promptly after school each night and excelled in extracurricular activities. There were scads of kids in my class smoking dope, having sex, and skipping school on a regular basis. I wasn't doing any of that. I just wanted to spend an afternoon with Mrs. Benfeldt, whom I hadn't seen since she'd left the summer before. Nonetheless, Mom held firm.

Seeing Bennie, even for those few moments, and landing the Eagle were the high points of my ninth-grade year, but by February 1975 the gymnastics season was over and I had less to do before and after school. I did not relish the increased time at home with Mom. Her relationships at work continued to crumble and she began harboring a great deal of mistrust for her coworkers, prompting her to be short-tempered with Lisa and me.

One wintry Sunday morning, Mom got up, walked into the living room, and kicked me awake from a sound sleep on the floor of our apartment. I sprang to my feet clad only in underwear, to the sound of her piercing voice.

"Neither one of you lazy-ass niggers thought to get up before noon and bring me the goddamn Sunday paper. I suppose I'm not worth half a shit to you now since I told you I might just walk outta that goddamn job and not look back. The only thing I'm worth to you little parasites is the paycheck I bring home."

I looked at her in disbelief as I pulled on an undershirt and a light pair of pants. Still in my stocking feet, I opened the front door to a blast of frigid air and bent down to retrieve the paper to give to my mother. Standing behind me, she planted her foot on my rear end and booted me out the door. She then reached for Lisa, who had also been scrambling to get some clothes on. There on the icy walkway I watched Lisa being propelled out the door, in pajama bottoms, a T-shirt, and slippers.

Confused and beginning to freeze, we heard the deadbolt latch. Ashamed, and afraid to be seen, we spent the first part of the day in the laundry room of our apartment building. To pass the time and amuse ourselves, we invented complex stories to tell each other. In one such story the central characters were a bored, rich couple named Deirdre and Gerund. In our telling, "ennui" emerged as the overarching theme of their lives. Too much time, too many cocktails, too much money. Deirdre developed into a stuffy and detached socialite, overly fond of the word "wonderful." Gerund was constantly whining and talking and helping and insinuating. Eventually someone interrupted our storytelling when they came in to do their laundry, prompting us to walk to an apartment building across the alley to look for change under the vending machines in the basement.

With the dime she found, Lisa called her new boyfriend, Evan, a sweet white boy whose liberal parents liked Lisa quite a bit. Evan offered to pick us up in his parents' car. I didn't think I should go with her since his parents had never met me so I waited the rest of the day in that basement storage room and tried to think of a plan to get back inside our apartment. Lisa didn't come back that evening until about eight P.M., and we both walked back to our place and tried the door. It was unlocked and we walked inside, sat on the couch, and began to watch TV.

Mom did not come out of her room that night, nor did she say anything about the incident the next day as we prepared for school. That evening, it was business as usual as we all sat down and ate dinner.

The arduous winter of 1975 finally passed. The sun returned and the days became warm. The thought of graduation from Everett Junior High sickened me. That last day of school everyone ran around like prison escapees, screaming their heads off and playing all sorts of pranks. How in the world could they be celebrating? I walked the halls saying good-bye to every teacher who'd meant anything to me in those three years. Mrs. Curran, the art teacher who always indulged my wisecracks; Mr. Friesen, whose mustachioed face guided me through geometry-phobia; Mr. Little, whose good-natured attempts to introduce us to the most delicate of subjects made his sex education classes standing room only; Miss Larkin ("Ruth," or "Ruthless," depending on our mood), who believed that any student could excel in algebra; and Mr. Steinke and Mr. Brestel, whose progressive approach to teaching English and current events helped shape the leftist views I hold to this day.

Leaving all of those good people behind, I could not imagine that life at Lincoln High School could come anywhere close to junior high. I had been told that high school would be the best time of my life, that it would be the last time I could be a "carefree child," and also have some adult privileges, like driving, partying, and going to football games. "All of the privilege, none of the responsibility" was what everyone said made high school special. Between scavenging cigarette butts and pop bottles, rehearsing lies to frame landlords, and walking to the pay phone before school to call in sick for my mother, I couldn't imagine what life would be like without responsibility.

MAMA MAY HAVE

❧

A s *Mom continued to* teach at LOMR, she began to complain more and more about perceived insults and slights at work. "I'm sick to death of changing diapers. I'm a goddamn teacher! Those worthless aides are supposed to change diapers, but they think they can foist that shit off on me just because I'm a nigger. It never ceases to amaze me how every goddamn aide in the place evaporates when they smell a turd," she'd rant. Lisa and I found these complaints tiresome. We saw signs of her slipping back into insanity, but we hoped that she could keep working through our high school years.

Listening to Mom rail in the next room, Lisa and I began to tentatively plan our own futures. At sixteen, Lisa had begun a work-study program for low-income kids, which paid a small amount for assisting her journalism teacher, Mr. D, in the darkroom after school. She worked a couple of hours each afternoon, and for the first time in her life she had a little spending money that had not been either scrounged on the streets or given to her by Mom. She paid for her own lunch tickets, school supplies, and clothes. She even gave me a little money every now and then. At fifteen, I had to get a work permit from the county and written permission from my mother to get a paying job outside of school. I was nervous about asking my mother for the note as new ideas, however practical, were difficult for her to accept. I figured my best strategy would be to apply for the job first and then secure permission from the county and my mother. I went to the closest and most familiar place I knew to look for my first job—Bronco's Restaurant. I'd heard they were looking for help and also that the minimum wage had just been raised to two dollars per hour. That was all the incentive I needed, so I scheduled an appointment with the manager.

My hands shook as I explained that I would like to begin working immediately. "Can you go down to the county on Monday and get your food handler's permit?" he asked.

"Yes," I replied eagerly.

"How about the parental consent and work permit?" he asked. "Do you think you can get those to me pretty quick?"

"Yes, I think so," I said.

I had already mentally prepared my speech to Mom as I walked in the front door and waited for her to return from work. "Guess what, Mom?" I gushed after I'd given her ample time to settle into her chair and set the TV tray in front of her. "I got a job, and it's at our favorite restaurant, and it's only a block away!"

Disgusted, she began to grill me. "What in the world do you mean, 'You got a job'?" she snarled.

"It's at Bronco's, Mom. We're there practically every night anyway.

I might as well get paid for it," I reasoned, repeating the most salient points, trying to make it sound as appealing as possible. "Jodie Weitzman's sister, Julie, worked there last summer and she *loved* it." Then, I began to filibuster with, "Tons of other kids from Everett work there and they all say it's *sooooo* cool. They're gonna pay me two dollars an hour, so I'll be able to buy all of my own school clothes next year like Lisa does and you can save your money to buy something neat for yourself if you want!"

"Lisa works at school, not a burger joint! Going to a job is vile. It is an abomination. I wish to hell none of us ever had to do it," she spat.

"But, Mom," I begged, "I *want* to do it. It'll be too cool, and the manager is *really* nice and he says I can eat a meal for free every day that I work. He said I could take food home for my family at an employee discount. I could just bring a bag home every night for all of us, and you'll never have to cook again. You can stop giving me an allowance!" I practically shouted.

That was what did it for Mom, I'm pretty sure. She had complained earlier that week that "feeding teenagers was like throwing money down a well," and had gone on and on about "the amount of money I donate to that goddamn clip joint down the street." I could sense my logic was not entirely lost on her and felt her resistance melting away and she finally relented with, "Go on if you must, but don't think it's going to be fun."

To me, bringing home a paycheck meant freedom. It meant that if necessary, I'd at least be able to buy a hot lunch at school and clothe myself, which I knew was a big deal in high school. Even after giving permission, I saw Mom struggling with internal conflicts about having both her kids working and no longer completely beholden to her.

I thought she'd welcome having some of the economic pressure lifted from her. She had always told us what a burden we were. On top of the financial burden, she suffered the interminable drivel of self-absorbed teenagers. Our mere presence seemed to be the greatest insult life had visited upon her. She bristled when we retrieved our school clothes from her bedroom in the morning. She was impatient when we told her about our school days.

A few days after Mom gave me the go-ahead, I stood at the cash register behind the counter at Bronco's with the manager, Wally, at my side instructing me how to count back change to the customers. After a few tries I mastered the skill and began working at the register by myself. Two weeks later I had a paycheck for more than sixty dollars. I walked on air to Klein's Grocery and placed it proudly in Mr. Klein's hands to cash. "This one's made out to you!" he said in surprise as I fumbled in my purse for my student ID. "Hey, I know it's you, kid, put that thing away. I'll be darned, I guess we all gotta grow up sometime, don't we?"

"Yessir." I smiled as he counted out three crisp twenties and some smaller bills. As I left the store he called out to his customers and cashiers, "Make way, ladies and gentlemen, we got a wage earner here. Comin' through!" By the end of that summer I'd worked as many shifts as I could and saved more than four hundred dollars. Even after I paid for my school clothes I still had around three hundred squirreled away. Several weeks before school began, I tried out for the high school volleyball team, paid for my own mandatory physical exam, and coughed up my own registration fees. Life was good.

THE LINKS
WE ARE

∝

I *dreaded the agonizing* walk to the "wailing wall," where coaches posted the names of all the students who'd made the cut for the team and advanced in the tryouts. I'd been practicing for three weeks with other sophomores and learning the fundamentals of the game, hoping to be chosen to play on the JV volleyball squad. I'd passed the previous two cuts and this last hurdle still remained. I'd told my boss at Bronco's that I'd need to cut down to weekends only in anticipation of making the team. So many girls had shown up for practice that more than half of them had to be winnowed out.

Two lists were posted on the wall that day. The first list had the names of the girls who'd been cut. The second had those of the final twelve who would remain on the team. I forced myself to look at the second list. Amazingly it contained my name. Because I was standing with a cluster of other hopeful girls, I suppressed the urge to jump up and down squealing in delight, but I was ecstatic.

Our first game took place my second week at Lincoln High. Our coach, Miss Nulte, had drilled us on the fundamentals: "Bump, set, spike it! That's the way we like it!" At five foot three I was one of the shorter girls on the team, but I was determined to hustle and never let the ball hit the floor. More often than not, I succeeded, and this made me a valuable player. I was crestfallen whenever I was benched and would do everything within my power to avoid that axe. The varsity girls had a good coach, too, but I preferred the hard-edged, no-frills style of Miss Nulte. In the two seasons that I played for her, we traveled to nearly every town in Nebraska, and we never lost a match.

Being a member of that team gave me purpose and community at Lincoln High School. Each day I waited anxiously for the bell to ring so I could bolt down to the gym, throw on my sweats, and start preparing for the next match. The girls on the squad became like family to me, and I made some of my closest friends on that team. After practice we would shower, dress, and sit on the bleachers to watch the JV boys play basketball. We'd giggle and point and gossip about each boy. Before long, we noticed some of them looking back at us, particularly after they'd made a basket or completed an impressive defensive maneuver.

One day Martin McLane took notice of me and asked to walk me home. I'd been watching Martin for some time and I liked the way he conducted himself on the court. It was clear to me that he preferred winning to losing, but he never seemed overly aggressive or competitive as did some of the other boys. If someone cut him off or fouled him as he ran down court, he usually shrugged it off or playfully "retaliated" on the next drive. I noticed he had a mass of scar tissue running the length of the backs of his legs and often wondered what had happened.

"Hi," he said to me shyly, as he headed to the boys' locker room. "Did I do okay out there?"

"Yeah, not bad," I smiled.

"Hey, if you give me five minutes, could I maybe walk you home when I get out of the shower?" he ventured hopefully.

"Yeah, okay," I said.

"Is Doug Quarrels gonna kick my butt if he sees me with you?" he continued, half-jokingly.

"Oh, I don't think so," I answered half-truthfully.

Doug had been making a point of coming to my locker after class and escorting me to the gym. I liked him just fine but could find very little fertile ground when it came to conversation. Doug liked football, basketball, and baseball, and that about summed it up. His goofy smile charmed me, but once we'd gone over the weekly sports scores, there'd been little else to talk about. To Doug, our lack of communication hadn't been a problem, and his face fell when he saw me leaving the gym with Martin.

"Don't you think you'd better tell him something?" Martin said anxiously, glancing Dougward.

"He'll get the picture," I said, flippantly. I could think of few less pleasant tasks than explaining to Doug why I wanted to spend time with another boy. Avoidance, though certainly not the best option, looked pretty good to me at the time. Doug eventually "got the picture" and moved on without incident.

That warm September day in 1975 marked the beginning of my falling head over heels for Martin Patrick McLane. I was "sprung," as they say. By October we were inseparable as we conjured up reasons to meet in the hallway between classes. He danced with me when K.C. and the Sunshine Band blasted on the radio. His moves were outrageously uncoordinated, his legs and arms flailing every which way to "That's the Way (I Like It)." At school functions he dove unself-consciously into every dance he could think of, to my amusement. At pep rallies he'd grab the megaphone and trumpet, "NuhNuhNuhNobody messes with the Lincoln Machine!" along with the cheerleaders, who found him equally charming. He'd sometimes grab their pom-poms and pantomime a choreographed dance to "Backbone," our favorite cheer. I'd howl as he stuffed his jacket down the back of his sweats to exaggerate his backside. "My backbone hurt / my pants too tight / my booty shake to the left to the right / to the left to the right / to the left to the right to the left. / One two three four five Lincoln High / don't take no jive / six seven eight nine ten / jump back—gonna do it again." And then they'd repeat it.

Sheeva Billings had introduced the cheer, and as the first black varsity cheerleader at Lincoln High, she was enormously popular. She brought other cool urban chants to the squad that put us leagues ahead of all the other high schools in the city of Lincoln. No one surpassed us in the spirit department and "Backbone" was our all-time, hands-down favorite taunt. Watching Martin laugh and joke with the students as he moved easily through the world, I yearned to be as positive thinking and well adjusted as he. I couldn't wait to see him after school, and before long, I wanted to see him in the evenings, too.

As uncomfortable as things had gotten at home, I dared not tell my mother I was seeing a boy. By January, I was in deep with Martin and living in terror at the thought that Mom would discover our relationship. She hardly needed any excuse to attack me, and she never uttered words of support. One evening as we were watching the local news on TV, they mentioned my winning scores on our gymnastics team. I was beside myself with excitement, never having heard my name on TV before, and I gawked at the printed words on the screen. Mom grudgingly admitted, "Even Lincoln honkies have to take notice when a little nigger child whoops their kids' asses that bad." Why must everything be about race? I thought with irritation.

Being smitten with Martin, who was white, made me hyperaware of the word "honky" and the frequency with which my mother used it in her speech. To my surprise, she continued, "As much as I can't stand those honkies, I hope to hell you marry one instead of some simple-minded, ignorant nigger. The last thing I want for you girls is a life of servitude to some no-account, lying black fool that can hardly put a sentence together." Wow. Now that threw me off balance as I tried to figure out how in the world I could win in this equation. I wondered how my mother could be so fiercely proud to be black and yet be so drastically opposed to our dating others of our race. Thinking back to my junior high romance with Eldon, I then understood a little bit more about why she had treated him so shabbily, eventually running him off. She often claimed to hate bigotry by either whites *or* blacks, yet she routinely employed racial slurs herself. I hoped she would just stop there, but she continued further by asking us if "we had any little boyfriends at school yet."

As much as I wanted to lie, I figured I had to use this opportunity to mention Martin's name, since I hoped to go to a movie with him soon. The only time I'd seen him after dark was when I had lied, telling Mom I was going to work but instead meeting Martin around the corner in his mother's car. That meeting had both thrilled and frightened us as our kissing led to groping, which led to an excitement both of us could hardly stand. I'd broken away with difficulty at the last possible moment with my virginity just barely intact. The next day after school we talked about trying to obtain birth control so we could finally "go all the way" with each other.

As excited as we both were, we were able to make rational decisions about our sexual future together. We were only sixteen years old, and both of us knew without question that the last thing we wanted was a pregnancy. Right up until the "big day," we continued to discuss our options and to decide how we would proceed.

I did take that opportunity to tell Mom about my "little boyfriend," hoping to divulge as little as possible about the seriousness of our relationship. "Yeah, I know this one kid named Martin McLane who likes me at school," I said casually.

"Martin McLane," she'd repeated with some hostility. "Is he black?"

Oh here we go, I thought. Here comes the third degree. "No. He's a white kid," I offered noncommittally.

"His name sounds black," she insisted.

"Nope, it's Irish," I shrugged.

"Oh. Does he like school?" she prodded.

"Yeah, he's a pretty good student, and he loves to talk about politics."

"How so?" she asked.

"Well, like, he's really into Malcolm X, and Rosa Parks, and the Kennedys, and stuff like that."

She stopped there, ending the conversation with an approving "He sounds like a nice boy." I was surprised things had gone so well and vowed to bring the subject up again before the spell broke. Later that week I asked her if I could go out with Martin on Friday night. To my amazement, she granted the request, with the stipulation that I had to bring him to the apartment to meet her before we left for the movie. Martin and I spent the week planning the details—he would borrow his father's Buick rather than his mother's small Pacer.

After reviewing our options, we had decided on condoms as our method of birth control. Martin had gathered the nerve to approach the druggist with his request, which, to his horror, he had to repeat after stuttering the first time. The next Friday he picked me up promptly at seven. My heart jumped into my throat as I heard his knock on our apartment door. Mom lay on her bed in the next room as I ushered him into the living room. He nervously extended the flowers he'd brought. His hair was neatly combed, his face clean-shaven. I tried at that moment to see Martin as my mother would, and was relieved.

I heard Mom stand and begin walking toward us. "Hello, Mrs. Jones," Martin said, his voice cracking.

"Hello, Martin," Mom said warmly.

Now I was beginning to feel faint, desperate to prolong this good-will until we could exit. Why was this meeting so different from her meeting Eldon? She'd looked at Eldon as if he were pond scum when she asked him how old he was. His dark skin, budding mustache, and deep-voiced reply was all she had needed to condemn him. Could my mother be exhibiting some sort of reverse discrimination with Martin? With this single "hello" did she actually believe him to be a more qual-ified suitor than Eldon because he was white? Either way, I could not have asked for more than this painless introduction.

"Martin, you be sure to have her back by no later than midnight," Mom said with mock sternness.

"Yes ma'am, I certainly will," he replied respectfully.

We'd hardly gotten into his father's car before the groping and grinding began. Two blocks into the drive, I was nearly topless as we drove toward downtown Lincoln. I was glad for his father's large car and automatic transmission as he unbuttoned my blouse with his free hand while he steered with the other. We drove toward Antelope Park, a popular gathering spot for high school students. We reached the park in record time and began undressing in earnest. I wanted to move to the backseat but could think of no delicate way to bring it up as he began to lie on top of me. My right leg mashed into the steering wheel, and I felt him move against me trying to locate the right spot. By this time I was so aroused, I could hardly stand it and took matters into my own hands. Wrapping my fingers around him, I stuffed his penis inside me.

Shocked nearly senseless by the excitement that maneuver created, Martin gasped, "I've got the rubber, do you think we should put it on now?" At least one of us was thinking clearly. Somehow we disengaged and sat up, embarrassed and awkward. I was trying not to look directly at his member and modesty had made him cast his eyes aside as I sat naked next to him. We tried to maintain our passion as he sat up and searched his pants pockets, which were now around his ankles, for the condoms. He struggled to maintain his erection as he fumbled with the package. The condom in place, both of us resumed our original positions, I, lying down with my head against the passenger door, him on top, trying to avoid bumping the horn with my knee.

Afterward, we lay there some minutes in our uncomfortable poses, tickled pink with ourselves for what we had accomplished. Both of us were now nonvirgins and very proud. From giddiness to sweetness, tenderness overtook me as I buried my head in his chest and breathed in his scent. We lay like that for a minute or so, car windows fogged up, when I heard a slight noise outside the door.

Thinking it had been a twig falling from a tree above us, I did nothing to ruin the moment—until I saw a blinding light shining into the passenger window. The uniformed arm holding the light was attached to an officer whose mouth began to speak. "You kids know the park closes after dark?" he said gruffly. For chrissake the least he could do is turn that goddamn light off and stop staring at me for a second, I thought as my face turned crimson while I frantically scrambled for some article of clothing to pull over my exposed breasts and pubic hair. Martin pulled his jacket onto his lap, sat up, leaning back against the head rest, his eyes skyward, hands folded.

"How would you like me to give both your folks a call and let 'em know what you're up to this evening?" Officer Dickhead leered as I rolled down the window after covering myself.

"No sir, neither one of us would like that much," I said, forcing my voice to remain humble as the officer smirked at us. He's enjoying this, I thought, and that made me angry.

"What are your names?" he asked lazily, his manner suggesting that he had all night to toy with us.

"I'm Laura, and this is my friend Martin," I answered.

"You two seem to be real good friends," drawled Officer D. "Could I see a driver's license, Martin?" he asked with mock politeness.

"Sure," Martin said, irritated. I put my hand on his arm to calm him. I didn't know what *his* mom would do, but I was certain I'd never see the light of day again if mine found out about this.

"You sound a little upset, pardner," the officer said condescendingly.

I squeezed Martin's elbow and beseeched him with my eyes to respond politely. "No sir, I'm just a little worried."

"Oh yeah, what about?" the officer asked, feigning innocence.

"Well, my mom would be upset if she knew we were here and I was hoping not to have to tell her."

"Oh you were, were you?"

"Uh-huh," said Martin weakly.

"Well, we'll see about that," the policeman said as he turned and walked toward his cruiser, all the while shining his flashlight on Martin's driver's license. Martin and I heard some laughter coming from the radio as the officer communicated with his dispatcher. We looked at each other miserably as we found our clothes and pulled them all the way on.

A few minutes later the officer returned, still chuckling softly, with Martin's license in his hand. "Well kid, it looks like there's no outstanding warrants on you, and you seem to be driving this car with your folks' permission. Is that right?"

"Yes sir, it's my dad's car and he said I could have it tonight," said Martin, brightening.

"I tell you what. I'm gonna let you two go this time, but I don't wanna see you in this park after dark no more. You understand me?"

"Yes sir," we chimed in unison.

"Okay then, beat it," the cop said.

Martin turned the keys in the ignition, put on his turn signal, and pulled out of the parking lot at a snail's pace. As soon as we were on the street we looked at each other and laughed till we cried. I gave him five and we turned our attention to the road ahead, resolving to choose our spot more carefully next time. It was clear to both of us that there would be many more next times.

As it turns out we did have time to take in a nine o'clock movie that night. I mentally rehearsed the casual manner I planned to use when I walked back through the front door of our apartment. When I was certain my clothes were on straight and my Afro crisp, I inserted my key into the lock. The last thing I needed was to be interrogated by Mom about our date. Martin, who was always the perfect gentleman for my mother's benefit, accompanied me inside and told her that we'd enjoyed the movie and that he'd love the pleasure of my company again soon. Mom's eyes practically fluttered as she responded, "I'm sure Lauri would love that."

As soon as he left she barraged me with annoying questions: "Did he open the car door for you?"

"No," I wanted to reply, "but he did open my legs for me."

She was relentless. "Did he pay for your refreshments? Was he ever forward with you? What did you talk about?" Mom's eyes glazed as she disappeared into the romantic fantasy she had constructed for Martin and me. All my life I had been witness to her fanciful fugues in which she took refuge when our situation was most dire. I forced patience into my voice as I answered correctly each of the questions she put before me. I only hoped no primal odor would escape and nothing would leak down my leg as I stood there answering obediently. Thank God I wasn't wearing makeup yet, as I'm sure my lipstick would have been smeared halfway across my face.

"He seems like such a nice young man," Mom said with more cheer than I'd heard in a while. Perhaps she was remembering back to her own carefree dating years, before we came along. Lisa gave me a look that meant "I better get the dirt on your date," as I walked past her and into the bathroom, where I took a long leisurely soak. That night as we lay side by side, this time Lisa on the floor and I on the couch, I related the details of my date, omitting the real nitty-gritty stuff. Something told me that she and Evan hadn't progressed quite as far as Martin and I had, and I knew instinctively that this might be problematic since Lisa was my *older* sister. I needed us to stick together for whatever in the next few weeks.

We were sixteen and seventeen years old by then, and we had developed a keen sense of impending doom. We could tell from the change in our mother's LOMR stories that things weren't going well for her at work, and the day she'd locked us out of the apartment stuck in our minds. When she came home from work she would, more often than not, head straight for her bedroom, close the door, and glare at us if we dared to intrude to look in the closet or dresser. She began eating most of her meals in her bedroom. Lisa and I were both saving our money for whatever might come.

By early spring our intuition proved true. Mom came home from work one day fuming about the injustices those "goddamn LOMR honkies" had visited upon her. It was not clear to me whether she'd walked out or been fired, but I knew she was once again unemployed. "I'll burn that motherfucking hellhole to the ground before I let those white devils see me again. I hope I'm hit by lightning before I ever willingly speak to those pigfuckers again." My throat tightened as her diatribe escalated into a rage. She walked through the apartment grabbing plates and dashing them to the floor. Lisa and I tried to shrink and become invisible as she railed on.

Finally, she retreated to her bedroom, exhausted; I heard her lighter flick and then smelled cigarette smoke. Lisa and I put our heads together to commiserate. In many respects I felt much the same as I always had when we'd come to this point, yet there was one subtle difference this time. Without knowing it, I had been preparing for this for the better part of a year. While looking into Lisa's downcast face and hearing my mother mutter obscenities in the next room was disquieting, I did not feel hopeless, as I had in years past. I was frightened; yes, I knew our futures were uncertain, but I somehow felt empowered in a new way. Lisa and I talked late into the night as we always did during these crises and slept anxiously, yet something new had emerged.

HEAT

❧

In the coming weeks I continued to run track after school, see Martin, and pick up shifts at Bronco's as often as my schedule allowed. Having Martin to confide in about Mom's latest descent eased my mind greatly. He'd shake his head sadly as I described episodes far beyond his life in the comfortable suburbs of Lincoln's middle-class Havelock neighborhood. The only experience he'd been through that compared to my childhood was the event that had produced the scars on his legs and back. As we lay in each other's arms in his mother's car, he told me how, when he was four, he'd been lying in bed next to his younger brother, two-year-old Timmy. Their mother had put them down for an afternoon nap and entrusted them to their older brother, Sean, as she ran to the nearest supermarket. Martin, unable to sleep, had awakened Timmy and begun entertaining him by striking matches they'd found in the kitchen earlier that day. Martin lit one, then another, and then, somehow, the whole pack ignited. He dropped the pack onto the bed as the heat began to burn his fingers. In an instant they were engulfed in flames.

Sean, still in the living room down the hall, heard nothing unusual but began to smell smoke. He leaped from the sofa and ran into the hallway to see what was happening. By this time the flames had jumped from the bed to the curtains and were licking up the wall and blocking the bedroom door. Smoke billowed from the crack between the door and carpet. Scared witless, nine-year-old Sean sprinted down the hall, flung the door open, and was driven back by heat and flames. Martin stumbled from the bedroom in flames, screaming and crying as his mother entered the house. She pushed Martin to the floor to extinguish him, shoved Sean out to the porch, and ran back to the burning bedroom. By the time the firemen pulled Mrs. McLane from her flaming house, her hair, arms, and clothing were singed; her middle son, Martin, was a smoldering mass of burns; and her baby, Timmy, was dead.

That event obviously changed Martin's life forever. I had not liked Mrs. McLane at first, mostly because she had never liked me, but hearing this story softened me a little toward her. Both of Martin's parents felt that his dating a black girl diminished their family status, but it was his mother who seemed most bothered. They'd both been vocal about denying Martin the use of a family car if the express purpose was to "take that little nigger girl" around town. He always had to lie about picking me up for any planned outings and I resented them deeply for it. While their tragedy softened my disdain for both of them, I never forgave them for their opinion of me.

My mom loved Martin as much as his parents disliked me. He and

Mom were starting a regular mutual admiration society. We would shuffle into the apartment after a day at school and within seconds Martin and Mom would be engrossed in a lively discourse on philosophy and the classics. Most of the time I was convinced she liked him much better than me or Lisa. It felt a little strange to see her be so fond of another human being, but at least she didn't hate him.

There was nothing to hate in Martin's kind and tender nature. Once, when I joined him on a visit to Timmy's grave, I wanted to take Martin into my arms and hold him as tight as I could. He gently and lovingly placed the flowers we'd picked on the grave. "I love you, little guy.... I'm sorry," he whispered almost inaudibly as he blinked back tears.

Martin's recovery had been difficult. He'd suffered third-degree burns over much of his body and had not been expected to live. His case was published in many medical texts because of the groundbreaking treatment he had received. The horror he had endured made our social barriers seem trivial and insignificant. Perhaps that helped bring us together, I'm not sure; but Martin helped me get through the next few months.

Mom's last paycheck from LOMR helped us scrape by until the end of the school year. I told my track coach that I wouldn't be able to practice much anymore since I had to start working a lot more hours at Bronco's, because my mother had lost her job. He was sympathetic and told me that I could still come to the meets if I practiced the long jump and hurdles on my own. I promised to do so and we left it at that. I'd gotten tight with the girls on the track team and they knew I was going through hard times. Sheeva Billings of "Backbone" fame was on my 440 relay team and helped keep my spirits high as I tried to juggle work, school, and my mother's violent mood swings at home. Kathy French, my former gym teacher, sometimes called to say hello, and I let her know my mom was getting pretty "weird," but I didn't elaborate.

On the last day of school my sophomore year, I dreaded the

prospect of spending the summer with my mother in that tiny apartment, breathing her smoke and listening to her fume. I asked for as many hours as I could get at Bronco's and applied for a second job at Burger Chef. I figured I had whatever it took to work any minimum-wage job Lincoln had to offer, and so did they. I got the job and devoted myself to working sixty hours a week. Strangely enough, my mother never brought up the possibility of Lisa and I splitting the rent, but I was certain it was coming to that.

Midsummer, when I knew she was nearly out of money, our situation turned awful. Lisa had gotten a job as a file clerk at State Farm Insurance and was as relieved as I to have an excuse to get out of the house. Though we were hardly ever home, our presence, when we were, irritated our mother. The second we walked in the door, Mom would light into us for the slightest transgression. I came home from work one day to find her sitting in the living room, chain-smoking and waiting for me.

"Where's the stopper for the kitchen sink?" she asked, pleasantly.

"I dunno." I shrugged.

"I've been looking for it all goddamn day, you little fuck, and I want to know what you've done with it!" she demanded.

"I haven't seen it, Mom. Really, I don't know where it is," I said, trying to maintain my composure.

"Well look for it, ass!" she seethed through her teeth.

"Okay," I whispered, just as Lisa was walking through the door.

"I suppose you 'don't know' where it is either," she bellowed at Lisa, who hadn't a clue what she was talking about.

"Uhhhhh," she said, stalling for time.

"*Uhhhhhhh,*" Mom mimicked cruelly. Mom clouted me on the back of the head as I walked past her and into the kitchenette. Surprised and hurt, I scanned the tiny room. I almost choked when I saw the stopper sitting right there in the drain, nestled in its usual place.

"It's right there," I shouted, perplexed and hysterical, as she stood behind me glaring daggers into my back.

"What the hell do you mean, 'it's right there'?" she screamed, mocking me.

"Can't you see it?" I said, pointing directly at it. "It's right there in front of you."

"That's a goddamn lie. What kind of a fool do you think I am? Where have you hidden it?"

A chill ran up my spine as I realized she really couldn't see it. She saw me, the countertop, the sink, the dish drainer—everything else, it seems, but the stopper. I picked it up and waved it at her, in a last ditch effort to bring her to reason. "Mom, it's right here in my hand."

A gasp issued forth from her as she sputtered, "How did you do that?"

"Do what?" I asked, totally confused.

"Where did you get that from?" she persisted.

"It's been sitting in the drain all day long," I replied, trying not to sound incredulous.

"You hid it and then you put it back...didn't you?!" she kept shouting.

"No, Mom, I didn't."

Angrily, she stomped into her bedroom, slamming the door behind her as I looked over at Lisa, who'd been completely mute until then.

"She's really wiggin' now," Lisa whispered to me.

"*Oh*, yeah. I really don't think she could see it," I replied. I began to formulate a plan of action that would be different from any other in our history of coping with our mother's mental illness.

PASSAGE

❦

"Yes, ma'am, we're both students," I said, trying to sound mature and confident. "Yes, just the two of us would be living there," I continued. "Oh yes, we've both got very steady jobs." I made every effort to sound eager but not desperate as I answered all of the questions Mrs. Fallberg hurled at me. I'd called her from a pay phone in response to an ad I'd seen in the *Lincoln Sunday Journal* about an apartment for rent a mere block from Lincoln High School, where I would begin my junior year in a matter of weeks.

I knew she was assuming that Lisa and I attended the University of Nebraska and I did not want to have to explain to her that both Lisa and I were students at a local high school. "Well, you certainly sound like nice girls. Well brought up," Mrs. Fallberg said maternally. "I need to discuss this with Mr. Fallberg, but at this point things look very good for you and your sister—Lisa, is it?"

"Yes ma'am, it is Lisa."

"Good, I'll call you back this evening if that's all right. What's your phone number?"

"Oh. I work this evening, ma'am. Would it be all right with you if I called you on my break at seven?"

"Oh surely, that would be fine," Mrs. Fallberg said gaily. I was glad I'd dodged the chance of her calling me at home. I couldn't risk my mother overhearing *that* conversation.

Lisa was apprehensive when I broached the subject of renting our own place after the "stopper incident." "C'mon, Lisa . . . let's just see if we can even get someone to consider renting to us," I'd cajoled. It was obvious she was wary of finishing her last year at Lincoln High from the uncertain shelter of our own apartment. "Look," I said, "we know things are just going to get worse. They always do. You saw her deck me when I walked by her to look for that stupid stopper. You and I both know it was right there in front of her face. I've never seen her freak out like that before. It's like it was invisible to her."

"Yeah," Lisa agreed uneasily. Even though I was correct, she wasn't yet willing to concede that our most viable option was to move out of our mother's house. "She might get a job pretty soon," Lisa said, faking optimism.

"She's not going to get a job. She's gonna keep freaking out until they come and get her," I said with finality.

"Yeah, I guess you're right."

"Look, Lisa, I called this lady today who thinks I'm the Messiah. It's in the bag. All *you* gotta do is be close by to get on the line and blow some smoke her way when she wants to talk to my sister. I'll do the rest," I assured a nervous Lisa.

"Well . . . okay," she finally agreed. "But if she doesn't wanna rent to us, let's just drop it, okay?"

"Yup, we will, I promise."

That night Lisa and I snuck out to the pay phone, telling our mother we were going to Bronco's to get some dinner. After asking her if she wanted us to bring her back something, Lisa and I left to call Mrs. Fallberg. To my dismay, Mr. Fallberg answered the phone on the first ring with a gruff "Y'ello."

"Hello, I'm Laura Jones and I talked with Mrs. Fallberg earlier today about an apartment that I believe you have for rent on Nineteenth and J Street."

"Uh-huh, that's right, it is still for rent. Mrs. Fallberg told me about you girls. So, you two are sisters, huh?"

"Yes sir, that's right."

"So, what classes are you two taking at the U?"

"Ummm, I've got a history class, and some English and a little bit of math," I answered, hoping I sounded convincing. I wasn't even sure what they called classes in college but I was damn sure going to try to pull this off.

"Well, that's just great," he said with gusto. "Our girls went to school there, too. How are your grades?"

"They're real good, sir. I haven't been there long, but I'm doing really well." He began speaking in a way that let me know Lisa and I had the place. We hadn't even filled out an application. He hadn't even asked us for job references or past landlord referrals.

"Mrs. Fallberg and I are retired and we don't get over to the place all that often, but if you girls can come to our house in Piedmont next Thursday, say noon, you can get a key and give us a fifty-dollar deposit and the first month's rent."

"Oh yes, that would be great," I said, suppressing the urge to scream my excitement. My heart pounded as I looked at Lisa and beamed. "We got it! We got it! We got it!" Both of us jumped up and down and hugged each other as we stood outside that pay phone and tried to imagine what it would be like to live on our own. How would we ever keep such a huge secret from our mother until moving day?

How would we deliver the news that we would be leaving her? When we were little Mom used to tell us she had eyes in the back of her head and that she always knew what we were doing. That had been enough to keep us honest for years. Of late, we had grown accustomed to withholding troublesome news, but this news seemed too huge. We tried to wipe the grins off our faces as we walked back home and pondered our futures. By this time, Lisa and I had a combined savings approaching a thousand dollars, which was more than our mother had ever had. The days crept by as we pulled double shifts, and I rushed from one job to another, trying to save as much as possible before the big day. I pushed thoughts of breaking the news to Mom out of my mind as I concentrated on getting to Thursday. The day dawned, and Lisa and I took two buses to get to the Piedmont neighborhood. We'd heard about Piedmont for years and had seen pictures of it on TV, yet had never actually been to what was widely held to be Lincoln's premier upscale neighborhood. Frantic that we'd be late, Lisa and I ran down the unfamiliar streets toward the Fallbergs' house.

Winded, yet determined to appear calm, I knocked on the door. Both Fallbergs stood in the entry as they opened the front door, which had not been locked. Their mouths flew open simultaneously as they gazed down at me and Lisa. "Hello, are you Mr. and Mrs. Fallberg?" I asked cautiously.

"Yes," they said in unison.

"I'm Laura and I called last week. This is my sister, Lisa."

"Oh, my heavens no!" exclaimed Mrs. Fallberg, either unwilling or unable to hide her shock. They did not offer to let us into their home as we all stood awkwardly, saying nothing, on their front porch.

Mr. Fallberg appeared on the verge of a heart attack as he finally spoke. "The missus and I have *never* rented to coloreds. Our place is a clean place with good tenants we've had for years. I just don't know how they're gonna take it. I don't even know how I'd break it to them. You never mentioned when we were talking on the phone that you were colored. Why didn't you tell me?" Mr. Fallberg accused.

"Well, you never asked me, and we didn't know that it would matter," I answered, deflated. "We've already given notice at our other place and I don't think we could find anyplace else this late," I ad-libbed. At this point Mrs. Fallberg asked if she and her husband might excuse themselves for a moment and they went inside their house and discussed the situation in private.

I gazed over at my sister, whose eyes were cast to the ground. I noticed how very large her Afro had grown and how very dark she must seem to this lily-white pair. My own Afro was much bigger than it had ever been, yet it could have passed as a perm. My skin was deceptively pale and I wished I'd found some sort of canard to come to this house alone, without Lisa. "We are so fucked," I said to myself over and over as I stood quietly waiting for a response. Eons later the two reappeared at the door. It was Mrs. Fallberg who spoke as her husband stood behind her. "My husband and I both feel that the two of you should have let us know over the phone that you were colored. However, we did promise you the place, and you did say you'd have trouble finding another apartment this late. As I say, we've never rented to coloreds, and we don't know how the other tenants will take it, but we're not the kind of people who go back on our word. Here are the keys."

The year before I had studied Greek mythology in school, and I now fully understood the term "Pyrrhic victory" as I took those keys. I couldn't think of a thing to say that would make any of us feel better. We concluded our visit with quiet "thank you"s as we turned and stepped off their porch and into our adult lives. Retracing our steps back to the bus, Lisa and I invented colorful scenarios with the Fallbergs to make us feel better about the whole affair. "We should have borrowed five or six pickaninnies in diapers and a few big black bucks to really scare the shit out of her. Can you just see them as we pulled up looking like the Beverly Hillniggers and spilling out of some pimpmobile!" I said to her. "Oh hell yes, and we'd drop buckets of fried chicken and watermelons on the ground as we tried to walk and beat our kids at the same time," she answered.

We figured we wouldn't be seeing much of either of them now that we'd been given the keys, and that allayed many of our fears as we rode the bus home. We were wholeheartedly committed to being model tenants—never late on the rent, always a sparkling clean apartment, and never loud or disruptive to the lives and routines of our neighbors, who we hoped would come to like and accept us. The only hurdle that now lay before us was telling our mother we were leaving, and this last obstacle to freedom weighed heavily on both our minds.

Throughout the next few days we agonized over just the right way to bring up our upcoming move to our mother. We figured we had three options: bravely telling her of our plans to leave, sneaking out in the middle of the night without a word, or chickening out of the whole thing to stay home and help her pay the rent. I was racked with guilt trying to imagine us refusing to help our mother, should she ask. It broke my heart to picture her alone in her room, obsessing about everything, Bible in hand, talking to God. Despite all the horrible things she had said and done to us over the years, I knew that, beneath the hostility and madness, she truly did love and care about us, and that it would hurt her to see us leave. It crossed my mind that of the many times she had left us, for whatever reason, she had always come back and at least tried to make us a family again.

Lisa and I were both bone tired of all her screaming, the paranoid accusations, the rage, and the hate-filled insults, but through it all we still loved her. Even so, I could not bear the thought of staying in that apartment at her mercy, waiting to be blindsided by another nightmare episode. Even if we paid Mom's back rent, there was still the possibility she'd do something so crazy they'd come and get us anyway. We knew that, at sixteen and seventeen, we were, in the eyes of the law, too young to be without adult supervision, and the thought of landing in another foster home or juvenile facility depressed us. Lisa and I could even be separated, which terrified me.

So we knew we couldn't stay with Mom. We had to tell her soon, but no matter when we brought it up, we knew it would be bad. Days passed as I wondered how to say the difficult words we needed to tell her. The opportunity finally presented itself the night before we left as I came home from Burger Chef to find Mom yelling at Lisa about some chore she'd failed to complete to her satisfaction. Again came the accusations of shirking our home duties and leaving everything for Mom to do, "since she no longer prostituted herself every day to put food in our mouths and clothes on our butts." "I just don't mean a goddamn thing to either one of you," she said. "Now that you can't bleed me dry trying to provide for you. I wish to hell neither one of you had ever been born. I'm sick to death of spending every waking moment with my ass in the air so you evil little shits can live in the lifestyle you think you're so motherfucking entitled to."

I knew I was next as I watched Lisa take it all in without saying a word. That we were both working full-time *and* doing our chores at home would not matter to her. In order to head off the approaching storm, I calmly said, "Look, Mom, I know you hate us being here and making it so you have to work at jobs you don't like, so me and Lisa got an apartment. We're moving out in a couple of days." A stunned silence ensued as both Lisa and Mom stared at me. Mom's eyes narrowed as she glowered with all the loathing she could muster, which was considerable.

"You did what?" she rasped as her lips disappeared and her teeth began to show.

I wanted to run out the door, but instead I looked balefully at her and haltingly explained that neither Lisa nor I wanted her to have to work so hard anymore to support us. I told her that the way we saw it, she could do anything she wanted to—"get a less stressful job or something"—now that we were getting out of the way and would no longer be there to burden her. I also told her that we were both sorry for making her life so miserable and hoped she could do something that made her happy with us gone.

For all of the times I'd fantasized of getting even and saying hurtful things to her while laughing aloud and skipping out the door, when the time actually came to say good-bye, I felt only sadness, love, and a tender sort of pity for Mom as she looked daggers at me and began to list the things we could not take from the apartment. Lisa and I had been squirreling away our clothes and personal belongings all week, and hiding them in the basement to retrieve on moving day, yet we still had no furniture, beds, or dishware to take to our new apartment. We figured we'd get those things from Goodwill after we got settled, so we were largely unconcerned with them until Mom brought it up.

"You're sadly mistaken if you think you're going to take the TV. I'll not let you take one dish or one stick of furniture out of this house. For all I care, you can starve and sleep on the hard floor wherever the hell you're going. That's what you get for thinking you're so motherfucking oppressed here. Well, you'll see, won't you. You'll see how I sheltered you from those pigfuckers all these years and kept those honkies away from you. You're going to *wish* you were here when you find out what those crackers are going to do to two simple-minded little nigger girls.

You'll see, just like I did—and honey, don't you dare think you're going to be able to get back in that door once you walk out of it."

Part of me was scared to death to be alone in the world without even one parent, crazy as she was, to at least try to look after us. Watching my mother struggle to "do for us" and trying to do for ourselves were two different things, and though I felt sorry for her, I wished she'd stop running down the list of all the terrible things that were going to happen to us now that we wouldn't have her around to fend for us. Up until then I'd been more apprehensive at the thought of returning to foster homes than living on our own, but now I was beginning to wonder. I'd seen the benefit of working outside the home and having my own cash, but actually paying the bills and keeping a job in order to survive began to tower before me. I tried to sound confident as I said gently, "We don't need a TV and we'll get dishes and other stuff secondhand. It won't be any big deal."

I said these things hoping to reassure her but she looked affronted as she roared back, "Providing for yourself isn't nearly as easy as you seem to think it's going to be. You'll wish to hell you'd thought this over when you see the mistake you've made. We could have lived here easily on what you girls make, but I see my presence here cramps your lifestyle. It's just too bad you've dragged Lisa into it too, but now you're committed so both of you get the hell out of my face and have a wonderful life." She stomped into her bedroom and slammed the door behind her. Lisa and I were left to whisper about how the revelation had gone.

Looking back, I now realize that some part of her was probably wounded, even though all she'd shown was anger. What looked like pure rage was likely, at least in some measure, pain. As we spent the last night with our mother, we tried not to let fear and sadness dominate our thoughts. We tried to dream of the possibilities and not the perils that lay before us.

IN OUR PLACE

❧

Our few belongings lay scattered about our new living room floor. I kept walking from one room to the next. Even though the Fallberg apartment was only one bedroom, it was larger than the place Lisa and I had shared with Mom. Originally our unit had been part of a spacious and grand old house. Even carved into four apartments, it held much of its original charm: large wood-framed windows with wide vertical-grain fir trim, a coved entryway between the kitchen and living room, and high plastered ceilings. I could almost imagine the workmen skillfully troweling the plaster over the thin strips of lathe that lay beneath the walls. The original glass in the windows had sagged and settled over time, lending images a funhouse-mirror quality as you looked through them. Martin, Lisa, and I grinned goofily at each other as we breathed in our newfound freedom. We hadn't even bought beds yet, though we couldn't have cared less. The place was carpeted and the padding beneath the rug would suffice until we could buy something suitable. Lisa and I laid our bedding out on the floor at opposite ends of the large bedroom. Martin looked dubiously at the arrangement and said, "Hey, I bet we could tie a couple of mattresses on the hood of my dad's car if I can borrow it in the next coupla days."

"Yeah, you think so?" I asked enthusiastically.

"Sure, I bet we could get 'em from Goodwill for next to nothing."

I tried not to get my hopes up as I thought about how Martin might have to lie his way into his dad's car. He had told his parents he was spending the night at his friend Chet's house and that had raised enough suspicion.

I made Martin promise to tell no one, especially his parents, that Lisa and I were now living alone because I feared the attention of well-meaning social workers. No matter how adult we felt, we were both still minors and not legally allowed to live without adult guardianship. His mom, though she felt I was beneath her son (which I often was!), would usually give her car keys up without too much whining or cajoling on Martin's part. His dad, on the other hand, was quite a different story. Mr. McLane put him through a litany of questions about where he was going, what he would do once he got there, with whom. Nonetheless, my spirits would not be daunted on this day, as we looked into each other's eyes with a gleam and wonder that said, "We really did it! We pulled it off!" As we lay spooning each other on the hard floor that night, Martin and I waited until we heard the sound of Lisa's snoring before we pulled our clothes off and began to rock back and forth.

The next morning, our hips stiff and sore from the hard floor, we awoke cheerily and tried to restore circulation to our legs. "I'm going to get you guys those mattresses today," Martin announced as Lisa and I looked doubtfully at him.

"We both have to work today, so we can't even help you. It's too much for one person to do alone. Let's wait till we can all go," I fretted out loud.

"No sweat, ladies. You just leave it to me."

I couldn't help but worry about him as I wiped tables and served up burgers all day. Finally my shift came to an end and I folded my apron, yanked off my hairnet, dove into the sunlit day, and started my walk home.

Halfway there I noticed a car moving slowly alongside me. I flushed with excitement as I realized it was Martin in his father's car with two clean twin mattresses tied atop. He pulled over, leaned toward the passenger seat, and tried to appear debonair as he grasped the lever to open the door. I jumped in and showered him with kisses as I asked him how it had all gone. "Oh . . . it went okay," Martin answered, evasively.

When he did not offer more, I pressed. "Well, what did you tell your dad to get him to give you his car?"

"Oh, I just made something up . . . it was no big deal. He bought it."

It was then that I noticed Martin was not wearing his glasses. "Hey, where are your specs?" I asked.

"Ummm, I guess I just forgot 'em," he replied, not looking at me. His smile faded quickly and I knew he was lying.

"Okay, what really happened?" I pressed firmly.

He looked at me as if he wanted to cry, and said softly, "He didn't believe my story. He tried to stop me from taking the car. He said he wasn't 'providing a taxi service for niggers' . . . and then I hit him."

Oh God no! I began looking anxiously around me, trying to see if there were police cars following us, or maybe his dad in his mother's car. Fuck, my mom had been right. Barely two days out of her apartment, and we were going to jail for assault and car theft...probably fraud, too, for not telling the Fallbergs we were "colored."

Martin started crying as he told me he couldn't believe his parents were racists. "We never really talked about anything like that growing up, and I just didn't think it could matter to them who I went out with, as long as they were nice and not into drugs or anything. I tell them all the time how smart you are, and good in school and in sports and stuff. I even showed them your name on TV one night when they gave the high school sports report. I just don't get it. It's like they won't even give you a chance. They just want to hate you." Martin wiped his nose on his sleeve and calmed down a bit. I listened in stunned silence as he went on. "A while back I told them you might be willing to give Shelley a few pointers in gymnastics. They're spending a ton of money on lessons for her, and she's just not very good. They were all for it before they knew you were black. Now they don't want you coming within ten feet of her."

I tried to suppress my own fear and anger enough to reach out and hold him. He laid his head on my chest as he described how he and his father had shoved each other when their frustrations had reached the boiling point. When his father jerked the glasses from his face, Martin had swung his fist reflexively and hit him square on the jaw. Horrified at what had transpired, Martin grabbed the car keys from the table and fled the house. "I can't let him call you that, Laura. I love you. He should be crazy about you, too." I petted his head and held on tight until his tears dried. We idled at the curb for some time before I asked how much the mattresses had cost him. "They didn't cost me shit," he grinned. "Dad paid for them. I used the money he gave me to register for football." We both laughed out loud as I imagined what his folks would do if they knew he was spending their money on Lisa and me.

As we drove to the apartment, a vague discomfort stole over me. As much as I wished it otherwise, I began to feel a twinge of resentment at the ease with which Martin could obtain the things he wanted and needed. He didn't have a job, and he had no urgency to get one. Besides mowing the lawn around the house, he didn't have to do much of anything to get the money his parents gave him. I, on the other hand, had to plan carefully, work, and save for every single thing. If I needed a new pair of shoes, I had to budget for them and perhaps work an extra shift. If my jeans were threadbare, I had to figure out how to replace them, while still managing to pay the rent and utilities. The phone that I called him on (when I knew he was home alone) was paid for by Lisa and me, not our parents. How could the disparity between my experience and his be so huge? We both lived in the same town, attended the same school, and had many of the same classes. I'd never gone on a family vacation, nor had I ever had a bedroom to myself. We'd never owned a home, and had rarely traveled by anything other than public transportation. I was terrified that his parents would have me committed, or fired, or expelled from school to get me out of their son's life. Who in the world would come to my or my sister's defense?

Martin had never seen the inside of the Nebraska State Hospital, never spoken with a social worker, never heard of the city mission, nor had he known what it was like to rely solely upon a parent whose mental faculties were so very fragile. He'd lived in the same house all of his life and had always been well-fed and clothed. If he had an earache, a cold, or some injury, his mother took him to the doctor. His teeth were perfectly straight and clean, while mine contained gaps and jutted at odd angles from my mouth. I'd never been to a dentist in my life, and the only doctors I'd ever seen had been at charity hospitals or free clinics. I remembered a time when I was five or six years old and had fallen on a broken pop bottle while playing tag. I'd cut my knee so badly the kneecap had protruded from the gushing wound. My mother was furious with me as we took a cab to the nearest hospital that would accept us. They stitched and wrapped it indifferently and told us to return six weeks later for them to check the bandage. The wound had become infected in the interim. Knowing my mother's tolerance for inconvenience, I remained quiet as the wound festered and my leg ached. When we finally returned to the hospital to have the bandage removed, the doctor stepped back at the sight and smell of it and told my mother the infection threatened to claim my leg. I recalled these memories bitterly as I sat close to Martin, my arm draped over his shoulder as he drove. I thought about our disparate realities and tried to quell an uneasiness as I fought the urge to blame him for his privilege. I squeezed my eyes tightly shut, trying to obliterate the image of Martin golfing with his mother on their favorite course. I reminded myself that they had lived through the trauma of the fire and losing Timmy, and that Martin himself had clung tenuously to life, so badly burned over a decade ago.

Both of us tried to be cheerful as we unloaded the mattresses and made the beds. Though there was no frame, no headboard or box spring, the comfort these mattresses afforded us was sublime compared to what we'd experienced the night before. As Martin opened the car trunk revealing that he'd also picked up a few lamps and some kitchenware, I began to feel lighthearted again. We started to make our apartment a home.

Lisa was ecstatic when she came home, and we reveled in our surroundings. She lay on her twin mattress with her arms behind her head and stared up at the ceiling. Martin and I did the same as we lay on mine. He told me he'd decided he was going to sneak the car back into his parents' driveway that night and then turn around and come back to spend the night with me. "I don't know about that, Martin," I said. "What if your dad's waiting for you, or has called the police or something? He might follow you back here and do something really bad, like turn us in. And it'll take you forever to walk back here from Havelock tonight." Christ, I thought, I'm beginning to sound just like my mother.

"I don't think he'd do anything like that," Martin replied. "Besides," he continued, "I just can't stand the thought of spending the night at home with them after what they said about you."

"Martin, I know you don't think they're capable of that kind of thing, but I bet they are and I'm afraid of what they could do to us." By "us" I wasn't sure if I meant the three of us, or just Lisa and me. I was really scared of them and I didn't know how far they'd go to get their son back.

I wanted to call my own mom and hear reassuring words from her, but I knew she'd have none. She had relented and been fairly kind at the last minute when we had moved out a few days earlier, so I didn't want to upset her about this latest development. She'd even given us her small color TV as we made our last trip out the door. Despite the nasty things she'd said earlier, her sudden concern for our well-being made my heart burst as we left our mother's apartment for good that day. I'd wanted to hug her and convince her that we'd be fine. But I'd begun to wonder if Mom's paranoia was instead keen insight into the world around her. Maybe I had been naive to think everything was going to be okay just because I went to school, worked hard, paid my rent, and obeyed the law. I watched Martin's skinny backside as he walked slump-shouldered out of our apartment with his father's car keys dangling from his fingers. He drove off, and I wondered if he'd make it back that night. Many hours later, as I lay in bed half-asleep, he returned and slid quietly in beside me and whispered that everything had gone fine.

"Were they up when you pulled in the driveway?" I asked.

"Yeah, but the TV was blaring so loud they didn't even notice me. I don't think they're going to come looking for me. They probably care more about the car than me anyhow," he replied.

"I hope so," I said, as I yawned and fell back asleep.

The phone jolted me awake, as it rang jarringly in the next room. I leaped to my feet and picked it up before I was fully conscious, mumbling a groggy "hello" into the mouthpiece.

"I know Marty is there. You'd better put him on the line right now, or I'm coming to get him and I'll be bringing the police with me," his mother caterwauled into my ear. I quickly tried to calculate if it was better to admit he was with me, or to deny it. Martin was even groggier than I as he tripped half-naked into the room, squinting at me. I pressed my finger to my lips, urging silence while I tried to devise a strategy. "He's there, isn't he? Answer me, you little black slut!" she shouted.

When I think back upon how I answered her, I am still filled with shame. It was as if I had wanted this one woman to pay for every injustice I had ever endured in my sixteen years. I could feel my senses abandon me as I spat out the words, "Yeah, that's right, you fuckin' bitch. He is here, and you better leave him here if you want him to be happy 'cause all you know how to do is kill your sons—whether you leave 'em in the house to burn up or you just torture them to death with your hateful fuckin' mouth. You get the job done one way or the other, don't you!" I screamed loudly as I hurled the phone across the room while Martin watched, horrified. Lisa was awake by then and saw the whole thing from the bedroom doorway. An awful silence engulfed us as we sat and waited for something to happen. Minutes passed before Martin said, "I better go home." I watched him put on his jacket, and he walked the five miles home.

IT'S ALWAYS FALL

✿

*I*n *the weeks following* my confrontation with Mrs. McLane, my relationship with Martin became strained and contentious. I'm sure my outburst was the chief cause. How could he possibly walk the line between keeping his parents happy and loving me? I often wondered how things had gone when he ventured home the night his mother called, but I couldn't bring myself to ask.

As if the problems with Martin's parents weren't enough to occupy us, Lisa and I struggled to juggle the demands of school and work. We dared not tell even our closest friends we were living on our own for fear of being swept back into the social welfare system. So awful was this possibility that our grades actually improved after we left our mother's home. We were resolved to be exemplary students so as not to arouse the suspicion of anyone who might be watching too closely. We subjected ourselves to a strict regimen. We awoke at six o'clock every morning, then set to work ironing our school clothes and work uniforms, combing our hair, brushing our teeth, and heading for school. I couldn't bear the thought of giving up sports, so I arranged my work schedule so that I could attend my first three classes until eleven A.M., jump on the back of Kelvin Mann's motorcycle, head to Burger Chef, where we worked the lunch rush together, get back on Kelvin's motorcycle, roar back to Lincoln High, attend two more classes, and then head down to the gym for volleyball practice. That year I was given credit for one class while I worked the noon rush at Burger Chef as part of the new work-study program. Often, I went back to work after volleyball to amass the hours I needed to pay my half of our expenses. Lisa, who had given up her extracurricular activities, began work as soon as school was finished. On weekends, when I had no games, I worked as many shifts as I could. I applied for a job at the King of Jeans store next to Burger Chef and began working there as well.

Conflicts in my schedule often threw me into a panic as I realized I was double-booked. Even though I'd inform my supervisors well in advance of conflicts, I regularly found myself scrambling to find a substitute for a shift I'd been erroneously assigned. My worst nightmare once came true when I discovered that I'd been scheduled to work both jobs simultaneously on the day of an out-of-town volleyball tournament. There were not enough hours in the day to fulfill all of my commitments and I felt enormously stressed. I was horrible to Martin, who would greet me with his usual sweet grin after school, which I'd return with a scowl. Moments later we'd be arguing. "No, I can't go to a movie tonight," I'd snap. "I know you don't realize this, but *some* of us actually have to *work* for a living." I felt ugly and mean when I said things like this to Martin, but I couldn't stop myself. It was as if I could not separate the kind, generous, sensitive individual that was Martin from the privilege that he enjoyed—and that I felt denied. I was angry at how hard I had to work and how little I had to show for it, and I focused a good deal of that anger on him.

Lisa noted my behavior with Martin and she wondered how I could be so cruel. She'd just begun dating a kid named Reginald Simms who was a year younger and lived with his family a few blocks south of us. I'd recently seen Reginald romping and cavorting with his younger brothers in their backyard, a muddy boy-space filled with bikes, toy guns, and clutter, and thought him childlike for his sixteen years. Sometimes I'd come home from school and find him sitting on the front porch, smiling broadly, waiting for Lisa. Reginald had chocolate-brown skin, a short Afro, beautiful teeth, and a deep affection for my sister. They got very close as the days grew short, the leaves began to turn, and the wind grew chilly.

On one such day I came home from school to find Mr. Fallberg stretched out on the floor of our living room with a can of varnish beside him and a paintbrush in his hand. He had not called ahead to tell us he would need to get into our apartment so I was startled to see him there when I opened the front door. He got up slowly and watched me as I entered the room. He did not apologize for his unannounced presence, nor did he make any move to hide that he'd been helping himself to a bowl of cherries I'd bought to snack on after school. As he got up he kicked over the can of varnish, which spilled onto a new leather purse I'd bought the day before to replace one that had fallen apart. I dove to salvage it while he stood by and stared at me in silence. I didn't know if the can had been overturned accidentally or on purpose. I only knew the purse had cost me much more than I could easily afford.

"I came here to start getting the place ready to rent," he said, finally.

Unsure of his meaning, I stammered, "To rent?"

"Uh-huh, that's right. You and your little friends gotta get out by next week. Me and the missus knew it was a mistake renting to you in the first place and now you got a colored boy with a gun scaring my good tenants half outta their minds, and I won't have it. We never rented to coloreds before, and we never will again." With that, Mr. Fallberg gathered the empty paint can, his rag, and his brush, and left. I found out a few days later, by talking with Reginald, that he'd sat on the porch earlier that week with one of his little brother's toys, waiting for Lisa to come home from work. That, apparently, was the "gun" Mr. Fallberg was referring to when he evicted us.

HOLDING COURT

L ess than two weeks later Lisa, Martin, and I packed up his parents' car yet again to move our scant belongings to the Floral
Court Apartments. From what we could tell, there hadn't ever been a
flower or even a shrub anywhere near the place. The old redbrick
building was one of three identical structures: A, B, and C complexes,
each possessing four floors and no elevators. The stale odor of cigarettes, cooking grease, and rotting garbage permeated the air. Because
the place was so run-down, Lisa and I managed to secure the one va-
cancy with little scrutiny, and even less money than we'd paid before,
but our new digs represented a distinct step down.

A few days earlier we'd visited our mother, who was on the verge of being evicted herself, and casually told her that we were "tired of liv-ing so close to Lincoln High School and having our friends drop by unannounced and thinking they could just hang out or crash there whenever they felt like it." Consumed with her own troubles, Mom bought the lie, which was a relief to me. I'd exhausted myself inventing ways to answer any questions that might arise concerning our sudden move from an apartment we'd adored days earlier. I feared most that she would try to convince us to consolidate our resources and find an-other place to live together as a family. I most certainly did not want that to happen. I kept telling myself that Lisa and I had suffered a set-back, albeit a big one, but not outright defeat.

My second worst fear was that I'd find myself unable to refrain from blurting out the whole, unedited story about the Fallbergs and Reginald and Martin's mom in one big spasm. My mother would then whip her-self into a maniacal frenzy, the only logical conclusion of which would be the annihilation of every white person in Lincoln, followed, of course, by our own suicides. But she only stared vacantly at the news. "Oh, that's nice, honey. Be sure and give me your new address and phone number when you get it," she'd said with little inflection.

Had I been more observant, I might have noticed how unkempt the place had become since our departure. Lisa noticed, and after we left, she wondered aloud if Mom had even gotten out of her nightgown in the last month. "You'd think she'd have all the time in the world to clean now that she's both unemployed and rid of us," she said.

"Yeah, I wonder what she's going to do when her unemployment checks run out," I answered. "Well, it wouldn't take much to get some funky minimum-wage job and pay the rent on that place," Lisa specu-lated. "We haven't had much trouble getting those kinds of jobs, and it's got to be a lot cheaper for her to live there without us."

We both worried that our mother's unemployment would lead to her eviction. It was frustrating to see her unmotivated and incapable of digging herself out of the hole she was in. Now that Lisa and I had been working for a while, we knew that low-level jobs were abundant in Lincoln. Our mother wouldn't have to settle for a job as a cashier in a burger joint or sales clerk in some jeans store—the jobs where they sent you home early when things got slow, and you wondered how you'd make up the hours in order to pay your bills. She had a college degree and that meant something. With minimal effort, we thought, she could make more than enough money to support herself. It baffled us that she did not take advantage of our departure and the financial freedom it brought her. It seemed strange to us that, not even six months gone from her home, Lisa and I were worrying about how she'd make it on her own instead of the other way around.

Already we'd weathered some tough storms and were beginning to feel our own power and strength living independently. As unsettling as the Fallbergs' ouster had been, we'd survived it, found another place, and remained largely invisible to the foster care system that had been so prevalent in our past. Among the few adults we'd told of our situation—Kathy French; my volleyball coach, Carol Nulte; and my English teacher, Merrell Grant—none had alerted any authority of our circumstances, choosing instead to monitor the situation closely by calling and visiting us.

It had been a huge leap of faith for me to reveal our true living situation to those three teachers. I had emphasized Lisa's and my commitment to maintain our high grades and to stay out of trouble. Seeing them as more than teachers, we confided in them, as it would have been too daunting to have no adult to advise us if things got really rough. They all promised to keep our secret, with the understanding that they were keeping an eye on us, and if things did get out of hand—things like missing school, sliding grades, or run-ins with the law—they would have to tell someone who would, in all likelihood, throw us back in the system. Those teachers were our safety net.

Heading into the long winter of 1977, Mom stayed holed up in her apartment and resisted looking for employment. However, toward the end of September, she began walking the half mile to visit Lisa and me at our place, usually on the weekends. Often, I would come home from work to find her stretched out on the ancient vinyl sofa that took up the greater part of our studio, reading or watching TV or chatting with Lisa. On one hand, I was happy to see her getting outdoors and into the world, if only to see us, yet it made me uncomfortable to note how comfortable she had become at our place. It made me nervous that she had no plan to keep her own apartment once her unemployment ran out and I tried to resist my suspicion that Mom scheduled her visits for when I was away. I suspected she wanted to isolate Lisa to work on her conscience and play on her sympathies. Mom knew Lisa would be the "softer touch," and therefore more likely to allow her to move in with us. I had grave concerns and worries about our mother's fate once her funds dried up, yet I could not tolerate the thought of all three of us trying to live together again. While the emotional and physical abuse my mom would bring with her would be intolerable, I detested, too, the idea of pretending I did not have a sexual relationship with Martin, which would be required if she moved in. "See ya, Martin," I'd have to say cheerily to him after we'd finished our homework, as I pecked his cheek and closed our apartment door.

I felt heartless and unkind. The guilt I carried was tremendous, but not so much so that I would give in should she ask to move in with us. The clock continued to wind down on Mom's unemployment benefits until she ran out of money and received an eviction notice from her landlord. By this time, she was not so much hinting as demanding that we give her shelter when her time ran out. She pitted my sister against me, pointing out how sweet Lisa had always been compared to me and calling me "a selfish little liar." She tried to convince Lisa that I was taking advantage of her by asking her to pay more rent as she had a better-paying job working part-time at State Farm Insurance. She also reminded Lisa, over and over again, of the sacrifices she herself had made to keep us in food, clothing, and shelter over the years. She told Lisa that we owed her, and that if I wasn't so selfish, I would be happy to have her live with us. Mom reasoned that if she moved in with us, she could protect Lisa from me, that together they could keep me in check while she stayed home and headed our household. When Lisa told me, I felt churlish and opportunistic. I *had* lately begun to exhibit some of the characteristics she attributed to me.

Recently, I had started dipping into the till at Burger Chef, which had increased my take-home "pay" considerably. While I was stealing far less than my coworkers, who had enlisted me to participate in the rampant embezzlement campaign, I felt apprehensive but also excited to be included in such a devious group activity. To most of them, who were still living at home, the stealing had been a game, a fun way to grab weekend party money. I considered my own theft to be somehow more noble, since I was stealing to survive rather than for sport. Nonetheless, I treated this money as a windfall, using a good deal of it to buy myself things that I wanted, like a guitar, rather than the things Lisa and I needed at home. While Lisa deposited a good portion of her earnings to our shared expenses, I used my ill-gotten gains to fund nonessential pleasures. I was more than happy to contribute the same percentage of my actual *paycheck* to Lisa, but I refused to share my extra loot. It wasn't fair to Lisa and I knew it, yet I continued. As if that wasn't bad enough, on my last visit to the public library I had come across an unlocked bright-red Schwinn LeTour bicycle, and decided on impulse to steal it. I had always wanted one but could never afford it, and I had grown quite tired of the unreliable Lincoln bus system. My mother saw the bike in our apartment during one of her visits and commented to Lisa that I seemed to be turning into "quite a little thief." She was right. I had developed a philosophy that championed the obtainment of anything and everything I wanted "by any means necessary." If the white kids didn't have to work for their toys, then neither should I. I had become bitter and cynical, and my mother, even at a distance from our day-to-day lives, noticed this change. She began to capitalize on this tendency and my many other faults to maneuver herself back into our lives.

I warned Lisa not, under any circumstances, to give Mom our apartment key or agree to house her for any length of time. I argued that our mother had had plenty of time to find a job and had chosen not to do so, a decision with which she had to live. Lisa appeared tortured when I commanded her not to answer the phone for the next few days, fearing it would be Mom pressuring us to relent. Throughout the entire ordeal I saw myself as a monster, incapable of compassion or mercy toward my mother and controlling and overbearing with my sister. I was all of those things, and I was aware of it, yet I did not succumb to my mother's demands, nor did I allow my sister to do so. When her eviction date arrived, Mom hurriedly found a job clerking at a local department store and obtained a short-term loan that made it possible for her to skip out on her back rent and move a couple of blocks away to a smaller, cheaper apartment. By late October that year, Lisa and I had made what we could of our tiny "efficiency" apartment and began to feel established and even somewhat comfortable in its narrow confines, relieved to have dodged our mother.

APPEARING
TONIGHT ONLY

⮜⮞

S ometime *before the* chilled air turned frigid and the streets iced over, Martin and I decided we needed a date to ease some of the tension into which our relationship had disintegrated. Martin had bought a copy of the *Lincoln Journal Star.* I flipped to the movie section, where I hoped we'd find something to our liking. My eyes fell upon a headline that caught my attention. It read, "Renowned Jazz Saxophonist Preston Love Returns to Midwest," and was subtitled, "Appearing Tonight Only at the Zoo Bar."

"Hey, Martin, there's a guy in today's paper that has the same name as my father," I said, trying not to sound too excited.

"Wow, that's weird. I wonder how that could be," he answered, equally confused. "Do you think it's his original band and that they've been together all these years and just kept his name after he died?"

"Maybe, I don't know. Let's read the article."

And with that we began to learn that this man, Preston Love, had been a local favorite musician and band leader until auditioning for Count Basie's band in the 1940s and embarking upon an international touring and recording career. Performances with Basie garnered him some fame and recognition in the jazz world, which he had parlayed into a lifelong career. That career, the article detailed, had led him far away from home and included some high-profile concert and television appearances with stars such as Johnny Otis, Diana Ross, Sonny and Cher, and the Jackson 5, among others. He and his family (*his family?*) had eventually relocated to Los Angeles, where he'd been on staff at Motown Records for the last few years.

I was totally bewildered. It was still unimaginable to me that any part of the story I'd grown up with about my father could be untrue, much less fabricated entirely. Scenarios raced through my head. Maybe the reporter had screwed up and forgotten to include the part about Preston's dying in a car crash in 1961. Maybe there were two Preston Loves from Omaha who played the saxophone. Maybe my real dad had been some embarrassing nobody with a name like Leroy McWashington whom my mom had wanted to forget. Whatever the true story, I couldn't stand not knowing it. Even though I was under the legal drinking age, I had to get into the Zoo Bar to get a good look at this guy, who just might be my father. I devised a strategy that I hoped would work and told Martin.

Moments later the two of us were heading downtown. A colorful scene awaited us, a typical Friday night in a college town in 1976. Scores of overstimulated, hormone-driven, newly emancipated students waited in lines outside popular bars, dressed in the standard uniform of jeans and T-shirts. Girls accessorized with gaudy jewelry, wide, low-slung, hip-hugging belts, and perfumes like Charlie and White Shoulders. Boys wore either Converse All-Stars or cowboy boots, depending on their social backgrounds. Hairstyles between the sexes were interchangeable. Long, shaggy, and parted in the middle. If a couple had gone someplace "fancy" for dinner, like Valentino's, the T-shirt would have been replaced by a shiny, colorful polyester shirt, guaranteed to stink to high heaven after an evening of dining, dancing, and drunken debauchery.

A crowd waited in the long line that snaked outside the Zoo Bar and led to the doorman inspecting their IDs. I asked Martin to park the car nearby and check my progress from across the street as I cut to the head of the line. Martin watched me unnoticed as he casually leaned on a bike rack outside another bar. I reached the bouncer and told him my story. I described to him how I'd flown to Lincoln from L.A. on a separate flight from my father and that I'd arranged to meet him backstage when I arrived. He looked at me suspiciously and told me that "my father" had not arrived yet and that, since I was underage, I could wait in a back room until he showed up. I glanced hurriedly back at Martin, who I suddenly realized had nothing to do for the next three hours, as the doorman escorted me into the tiny storage room next to the bar.

It was hard to breathe as I sat there waiting for this man, whoever he was, to arrive. I checked my hair and clothing every few minutes, hoping to be presentable enough to meet him. I had to pee but I dared not risk venturing into the crowd and being asked to leave by the bouncer. By the time the music was scheduled to start, I was but a distant memory in the mind of the doorman and I stepped tentatively out into the crowd.

There was hardly room to exhale, let alone dance, as I watched the band step onto the stage from an almost hidden door. A tall gawky white guy with a big, red jazzy-looking Gibson electric guitar walked out followed by a huge black man who positioned himself behind the drums. Next came a suave, middle-aged, medium-brown man with a modest Afro. He stood in front of the microphone and adjusted its height. Last appeared a light-skinned black man with large glasses who looked to be in his forties. From the moment I saw him, I knew he had to be my father. Jesus, I thought, he looks just like me. He walks like me. His hands look just like mine, with all the veins in the same places. Even his legs and backside look familiar to me.

Then, without an introduction, he and the band launched into some beboppy bluesy shuffle that sent a cheer through the crowd and had everyone up and moving instantly. I stood transfixed. How could this man standing in front of me have eluded me all these years? Could he really be my father? I hung on his every word and smiled at all of his jokes. He played his saxophone amazingly, yet he didn't seem to take himself or his music too seriously. He had an ease and style with his band that suggested they were all friends and enjoyed one another offstage as well. It looked like he was having fun up there, and he hammed it up for the exuberant college crowd. I didn't even know him, but I found myself wanting everyone to like him and clap for every single thing he said or did. I felt a kinship with him. When his gaze fell anywhere near where I stood, my heart pounded even harder in my chest, and I could feel my hands dampening. I could hardly meet his gaze as I wondered if he was actually looking at me, or just in my general direction. How could I summon the courage to get close enough to speak to him? What if he didn't like me or thought I was a geek? What if he denied any knowledge of me or my mother and sister? What if he was angry I'd come?

I was driving myself crazy with questions, so I just concentrated on what was happening onstage. Preston introduced Wesley "Mr. Blues" Devereaux to the crowd as the band launched into the intro to the Marvin Gaye song "What's Going On." That saxophone intro has always been among my all-time favorites, and hearing him play it was heaven.

Wes's singing voice was lovely and resonant. The room combusted when he called, "What's goin' on." Everyone shouted back, "What's goin' on," until the whole place reverberated with the phrase. The air was blue with smoke and the smell of sweat and cologne was almost overpowering, yet there was no place else I would rather have been. Not only was this the first bar I'd ever been inside, it was one of my first live concerts, and I was standing mere feet from the man I believed to be my father.

All too soon the song ended and Preston leaned into the microphone to announce that he and the band were going to take a short "pause for the cause," and would be back soon. I watched him unhook the saxophone from the strap around his neck and place it in the stand at his feet. Now what do I do? Should I approach him? He looked approachable sitting there at the bar, sipping a rum and Coke. He chatted easily with fans standing around him. I toyed with the idea of acting like I was just another college student, but I feared my resemblance to him would give me away. I finally decided, not without doubt, to go with the honest approach.

His bandmates, Wes and Hank, had joined him for a drink and I was nervous as I walked up to them. "Ummmmm, hi."

Preston's eyes fell upon my face as he drew the slender cocktail straw to his lips. "Hello," he said warmly, after a deep pull made a substantial dent in his drink.

"Um, did you ever know a lady named Wini, errr . . . Winifred uh, Winston or Jones?" I asked, feeling like a complete moron.

"Why, yes I did, young lady," he returned affably.

"Well, like, how well did you know her?" I probed, hoping he wouldn't take offense.

"Very well" came the rapid reply.

"Cuz, I think I might be your daughter, is why I asked," I blurted.

His jaw fell open and he placed his drink on the bar behind him. "Well, I'll be goddamned," he said, incredulous. "You sure are! Which one are you, Laura or Lisa?"

"I'm Laura. Lisa's at home. She doesn't know I'm down here. Neither one of us is old enough to even be in here."

"No, of course you're not. Let's see, you were born on January the fifth, nineteen-sixty, and Lisa was November thirteenth, nineteen fifty-eight, so that would make you just about sixteen now, wouldn't it?"

"Yeah, that's exactly right!" I gushed, almost delirious with excitement.

"You were just a little baby, still in diapers and barely walking the last time I saw you, and Lisa was just starting to talk like crazy."

I tried to imagine myself as a baby but found it impossible. My mother, during one of her breakdowns, had cut up or burned every picture of us as infants for some reason known only to her. I realized at that moment how odd it had been that she had never shared favorite baby stories with us as mothers often do, and that she seemed to have no fond memories whatsoever of anything we had ever done as small children.

"Your mother was the most beautiful thing I'd ever seen when she got off that train in Denver to play with my band. She was wearing a gorgeous yellow flowered dress and the way she tossed her hair around—like to make a man go crazy," Preston said, laughing heartily as he thought back to that moment. He sighed wistfully as he took in my every feature. "Look at you," he said, beaming. "Hank, don't she look just like me?" he said loudly to his drummer, trying to be heard above the crowd.

"Say what?" said Hank, obviously confused.

"Like me," he reiterated, louder this time. "Don't she look just like me? This is my daughter, Laura." Just hearing the words, "my daughter,

Laura," spoken by anyone other than my mother thrilled me beyond belief. A man had just called me his daughter. I never in my entire life expected that would happen, and now, here it was. I ached to hear him say it again.

Hank was huge and teddy bear–like as he pulled his bar stool closer to me and said, "Did you just say this is your daughter, Preston?"

"Uh-huh," he answered proudly. "Look at her skin; she almost look white, don't she?" he continued. "When she was born I looked at Wini like, 'Who else you been messin' with?'—but now, there's no mistakin' it. She's mine."

"Preston," Hank said, bewildered, "I ain't never known you had any other kids besides Norman and Richie and them. Is Betty they mama, too?"

"Oh, good Lord no!" Preston shot back, jovially. "And if she could see this one now, she'd probably whoop my ass from one side of Omaha to the next." He pronounced Omaha "Oh Mee Haw" to be funny and that cracked me up.

Hank gave me an affectionate wink as he said, "Oooh, I bet she would, too!"

It was beginning to feel like the most perfect evening of my life as I basked in the light of their attention. Before I knew it, Preston excused himself to begin his second set, leaving me there to wonder what my future with him held. My head swam as I began to consider the fact that Preston was *not* dead, and that Hank had made reference to other children and even another wife. Who in the hell were "Norman and Richie and them"? And was Betty someone Preston married after the divorce from Mom? I had so many questions and feared I would not get them all answered that night. It pained me to think that this man could disappear just as suddenly as he'd appeared.

Another hour of music flew by as I drank in his every word, note, and gesture. All too soon the band was done playing for the night, and

Hank and Wes and the white guitar player they called Slim had packed their gear into Preston's station wagon. I yearned to learn all that I could before he left so I fired questions at him. I asked him how long he had been married to my mother. For the second time that night, his jaw nearly hit the floor as he informed me that he and my mother had never been married. "Oh, heavens no ... I've been married to my wife, Betty, practically all my life—since we were kids. What gave you the idea we were married?"

"Well, Mom always told us you guys had been married for a couple of years and that you'd been killed in a car accident when we were just babies."

"Haaaaaa!" bellowed Preston heartily. "I'm telling you, I've never been married to anyone except Betty, and I sure as hell wasn't killed in no car crash, honey. You musta 'bout had a heart attack when you saw me walk on that stage healthy as a horse! I mean, I figured Wini was mad as hell when she left town with you kids, but I never thought she'd keep you away from me your whole childhood."

I was completely flabbergasted by these revelations, yet dared not interrupt for fear of stopping the flow of information about my past. He continued, "You know it didn't set too good with her when she found out that Betty was pregnant with your brother Richie at the same time *she* was pregnant with *you*. Norman and Lisa weren't even out of diapers yet."

"Sooo ... ," I said, assembling the pieces of this puzzle, "if you were married to Betty while you were on the road with my mom, and she knew you were married ... how come she was so mad at you? I mean, you told her you were already married, right?"

"Sure I told her, but things were different then," Preston explained. "I was so pretty back then. The women couldn't keep they eyes *or* hands offa me. A nigger had it made if he was clean and good-lookin' and could play something—horn, piano, tambourine, garbage can—anything. It didn't matter if you were married. They'd see our bus pull up and practically pass out. I had women all over the country. I know I've got *at least* seven other babies out there somewhere. I've had a lot of women, but Wini—now that was different. That was love."

A wave of contradictory feelings began to arise in me, alternating between admiration for Preston's candor and a growing repugnance for what seemed to be an all too cavalier attitude. "Yeah, I was crazy about her. She was not only fine, she was educated and 'hardly dated.' She was hot-tempered, and niggers had to act right around her! I mean, we had something real good—and I'm not just talkin' 'bout you know what—but that was good, too! From the minute I laid eyes on her, I knew I had to get next to her, and she felt the same about me, even if I was twelve years older. You can just tell when a woman likes you that way, you know what I'm talkin' about."

I nodded in agreement, but it struck me as vulgar and distasteful to hear him speak of my mother as just one of his many conquests. He continued, "Did she ever tell you about the fight she had with her boyfriend over coming out to sing in my band?"

"No," I answered, completely absorbed in his story.

"She didn't? Oh well, listen to this."

Preston seemed to be enjoying himself as he launched into his next story. "My lead singer had just quit the band, up and left, because she was messin' with one of my players and he wasn't behavin', so they got into it, and she took off. So there I was in Denver without a singer, and in those days you had to have a pretty girl fronting your band if you wanted to get any work. Preferably someone light-skinned, with good hair. You couldn't have no Moms Mabley up there. I was desperate to get someone so I made some calls around Omaha and someone told me there was a girl in Lincoln who looked good and could really sing. He hooked me up and I called her to see what songs she knew and could she read music. I could tell over the phone that she was smart and could do the job, so I hired her right then and there. She hopped on a train and got to the station about a half hour before we were supposed to go onstage. I watched her step out of that car and I thought I'd won the Kentucky Derby. That dress she was wearing—she was a knockout and she knew it, too. I kept thinking to myself, Oh, Lord, how am I gonna keep the fellas offa her. I picked her up in our rickety old tour bus and ran over the songs and she just sat there nodding at me. It wasn't till we got to the gig that I saw that she'd been hiding her hands from me the whole time we'd been talking. She'd stuck them in a muff and I couldn't get her to take her hands out of it so I could help her into the bus. I didn't see them at all until I handed her the sheet music with our arrangements on it. When I did see 'em, I couldn't believe it. There was cuts all over her hands and they were bleeding like crazy. Yeah, her and her little boyfriend, they'd had a big knock-down-drag-out about her leaving him to come to sing for me and he tried to stop her from goin'. She put her hand through a window tryin' to get that nigger to back off. I never saw such a mess. It musta hurt like hell, but she acted like she didn't even notice it. She just sat on a stool that night with her hands in that muff and sang like an angel. I had to make her go to a doctor the next day and get it cleaned up. I don't know how long she planned to ignore it, but that's when I knew that Wini was no one to mess with."

I wanted to break down and cry, imagining my poor mother young and alone, with all that glass stuck in her hand, but all I said was, "Gee, I guess she didn't want us to know all that."

"I guess not," he agreed amiably. After a slight pause he offered, "I think she truly believed that I was gonna leave Betty to be with her." He chuckled as he said this, as if it was the most ridiculous notion he had ever heard. "I knew Wini always thought she was cuter and smarter than my wife and probably figured she'd wear me down and eventually get me to go ahead and be *her* husband, but that wasn't ever going to happen. I love my wife and kids, and I've always been a family man." Clearly he thought of his "family" as something that did not include me, and of his "wife" as someone other than my mom. I began to realize that I'd been subconsciously entertaining a fantasy that we were all going to be a family now and Mom wasn't going to be crazy anymore.

Though I was sixteen years old and knew better, it had seemed plausible that we could just pick up where they'd left off in 1960-something, and move on together like the Brady Bunch. I found myself grappling with the contradiction of feeling kinship and warmth for this man—a swell, good-natured guy full of great stories—and the other side of me, which wanted to put my hands around his neck and shake him, screaming, "How dare you, you arrogant son of a bitch, walk out on my mother with two tiny babies and no money, and never even check to see how we were doing in over fifteen years! No wonder my mom was so crazy."

I wrestled mightily with the conflicting emotions I was having toward my "new" dad, Preston Love. I wanted to shout, "Have you any idea the havoc you've wreaked, fathering all these babies for which you seem to feel no personal responsibility whatsoever? Do you understand that you are responsible for the existence of scores of kids like me, whose whole lives have been full of nothing but misery and deprivation? Is it worth it, Preston?" But, instead of saying those things, I stayed calm, choosing to relish the moment of our reunion and be grateful for the wealth of information this man was giving me. By the end of the evening, I found myself unable to sustain much animosity toward him. For all his faults, he was pleasant and funny, easygoing and handsome. I wanted to love, and be loved by, him. I wanted his love much more than I wanted to confront him, or to hold him accountable for anything that had happened in the past. I wanted to matter to him, so that I could forever have access to his world and to my past.

☙

Somehow that night I was able to convince Preston and the band to stay a little longer at the Zoo, so I could call my sister from the bar and tell her what I was doing and with whom. As luck would have it, she was just arriving home after a date with Reginald when the phone rang. "Well, I'll be go to hell!" exclaimed Lisa. Martin, who had returned to the apartment after tiring of waiting for me on the corner, offered to drive her down to the Zoo to meet "Dad." Lisa had been just as excited as me to meet Preston, but she felt a little deflated after he asked Hank which one of us looked most like him. Hank looked from me to Lisa and back again, and said, "Gee, I don't know, Preston, they both favor you."

"No, Hank, look again, can't you see it?"

Hank tried again. "Uh, Lisa, I guess."

"No, no, no, look how dark she is, Laura looks just like me."

Lisa stared at her shoes.

Over the next few years, Lisa and I met Preston a number of times at the Zoo Bar and even sang onstage with his band. Not having sung in front of an audience since my junior high delivery of "Anticipation," I was both nervous and thrilled. I sang a rendition of the Ohio Players hit "Fire," along with other funk and jazz standards. When I teamed up with Wesley "Mr. Blues" Devereaux to cover Deniece Williams and Johnny Mathis's "Too Much Too Little Too Late," the joint went wild, a definite showstopper. I was overwhelmed by the reception.

Sometime in 1977, at one of his Zoo gigs, Preston came up to us at the end of his break and nodded toward two handsome young men whom we had noticed the minute they'd walked into the room. He said, "See those two over there?" I wanted to tell him that Lisa and I had seen nothing else for the last hour. "They're your brothers." Lisa and I looked at each other as we noticed them now noticing us. Preston waved them over and walked back to the stage before they arrived. We found them a place to sit and gaped expectantly at them.

"Hi," Richie said, invitingly.

"Hi," Lisa and I both sang back in unison.

Neither Norman nor Richie said anything else as Preston began his second set. Lisa and I nudged each other under the table, trying to determine what our next move should be. At a quiet point in the song, Lisa leaned toward Norman and blurted, "Isn't it great? We're your sisters!"

Norman's eyes doubled in size as he whipped his head around and gawked at her. He then leaned into his brother's ear and whispered something that caused Richie to do the same.

"Sure you're sisters," Richie said, trying to recover. "That's great cuz me and Norman never met any sisters in Lincoln before, hardly any brothers either."

Now my eyes were doing the widening as I imagined what he meant by "hardly any brothers." Did this kind of thing happen to them every day?

Richie continued, "Yeah, me and Norman was just sayin' on the way down here how much we hate comin' to Lincoln cuz it ain't nothin' but white folks. No brothers and no sisters." Oh, no, I thought, beginning to realize they had misunderstood Lisa's meaning.

"No," I said, "what Lisa meant is that we're your real sisters, not just 'sistahs.' Preston is our father, too!" It was their turn to gape as we both began to explain the situation. To our amazement, Preston had not told either of his boys about us, nor had he bothered to mention they'd probably be running into us tonight. With the introduction out in the open, the four of us began a lively discussion about everything and anything. Preston glanced down and smiled at all of us from time to time. After the end of the set, Preston walked out into the audience to mingle with his fans. He eventually made it back to our table and sat down. "Well, you all seem to be hitting it off pretty good," he laughed.

"We sure are," said Lisa happily. "We were just comparing how much we all look alike and telling them about our mom," Lisa beamed.

"You're doing what?" Preston shot back, alarmed.

I explained, "You know, telling them about *our* mom. They told us about Betty and now we're telling them about Wini."

"You mean you told them you're their sisters?" Preston asked, incredulous.

"Well, yeah—I mean that's okay, isn't it?" Lisa returned.

Preston shook his head in disgust and said, "No, they're too young for that."

We were able to recover from this shaky beginning. Every time Preston played in Lincoln, we met up with Norman and Richie. We thought them devastatingly attractive and worldly and spent hours together laughing and talking. Perhaps a year went by before Preston, Norman, and Richie accepted our invitation to see our Floral Court apartment. Upon first glance, Preston, who had been casting a critical eye on the surrounding neighborhood, proclaimed our apartment to be a "funky little dive." Though he'd said it affably and with no particular judgment, I was crushed by his assessment of the place Lisa and I had painstakingly spruced up for their visit.

I wondered what sort of house he and the boys lived in, yearning to be a part of it. I imagined it to be a modern, palatial, split-level rambler, like those I'd seen on TV shows like *My Three Sons* and *Bewitched*. But in the next instant I reminded myself that, at seventeen years old, I had been living on my own for over a year and no longer needed parenting.

At some point that year, Lisa and I began to press for an invitation to visit Preston, Norman, and Richie in Omaha, and perhaps even stay overnight at their place. Preston reminded me of his wife's delicate position and of her grudging acceptance of his philandering. He warned us to never call him at home for fear Betty would answer and be hurt and angry. He related a story to me of how my mother, Wini, had "freaked out on him one night" when Lisa and I were still babies, and had called him at his house. She'd shrieked at him that he'd better come over to her place, pronto, and "get these goddamn babies out of her face" right now or she was going to do something drastic. Unable to tear himself away from the needs of his own wife and sons, Preston had hung up on her with the admonition to just try and get the babies to sleep and get some rest herself. Unsatisfied with this reply, our mother had packed us up in her arms and walked the few blocks between her apartment and his house and deposited us on his doorstep on a snowy winter night. She'd knocked on the door and walked away, leaving Preston and Betty to deal with the squirming, squalling things on their front porch. Betty had gone off on him that night. Cowed into submission, Preston had meekly gathered us up and taken us to his brother and sister-in-law's house and left us with them until my mother could be summoned and persuaded to reclaim us. It was when he told us this story that I learned that I had been named for his sister, Laura Love.

I felt awkward and uncomfortable hiding myself from Betty, yet I also felt sorry for her. She must have endured many insults to her pride while married to Preston all those years. I didn't want to cause her to suffer any more than she already had within her community, which must have known of her husband's affairs. With some misgivings, we agreed to shelter him from her wrath and to contact him only at work. He told us many times what a good, loving, and patient woman she was and how she had stuck by him, even though his own reckless behavior had tried her patience. He also told us what a good mother she had been to their four children (two of whom we had yet to meet) and how much he wanted to avoid causing her any more pain.

After meeting my father, I realized my naïveté in believing that my family would be well and whole from that moment on. Our reunion had not been as transformational or mind-boggling to him as it had been to me. Our reactions to the event had been wildly different. Much time passed before I truly comprehended the notion that these sorts of occurrences, while once in a lifetime for me, may have been fairly commonplace to him.

SACRED WOUND

❧

W hen I was in my mid-thirties and a working musician myself, a woman came up to me after one of my concerts and told me that my father had written an autobiography that she had read out of her interest in my music. She had been appalled to note that he had never mentioned having any children other than those by marriage. The Laura Love that she'd read about in the book was his sister, whom he'd adored. She felt it was my duty as a woman to confront him and make him publicly accountable for this egregious omission, but I didn't want to take that route. Admittedly, it did hurt to be left out of his story, but in some ways I wanted to respect his obvious wish to hide the truth, so I chose to ignore the woman's advice. And, when it was sent to me by a friend, I also chose not to read the book.

My sister, Lisa, on the other hand, bought and read the book and found herself calling Preston, both to say hello and to ask why we had not been mentioned. He answered that his editor had felt it "unimportant to the story," and that it "detracted from the musical focus of the work." According to Lisa, the book contains many amusing anecdotes about his family background and history, some of which I am sure would answer questions I have about my own genealogy. None of these, I am told, make any reference whatsoever to the numerous extramarital affairs he had, nor the children that resulted from them.

As my own musical career flourished, I began to be asked regularly about my family and what my artistic influences had been. Reporters often questioned my childhood exposure to music, to which I responded that my mother had once sung in my father's band, but I hadn't known my father as a child. This answer often prompted more questions about him, which I answered as best I could. The more I told people of my past, the more I could see how strange and fascinating my story was to them. Sometimes I would realize, mid-interview, that I was expressing resentment toward Preston for not ever attending a gig of mine, for never showing me how to play an instrument as he had so lovingly done with Norman and Richie, for not seeing me graduate with honors from high school and, years later, from college—for not spending time with me.

Once I recognized my anger, I'd find myself trying to rein it in for the rest of the interview. Afterward, I'd think about the conversation for hours and wonder if I'd said anything that would hurt his feelings if it got back to him. Then I'd talk myself out of worrying about his feelings by convincing myself that he'd never hear of my career or read the articles anyway. I could not have been more wrong. Eventually the news of my success did reach him, as did my confessions of illegitimacy, bitterness, jealousy, and a family history of poverty and mental illness.

Sometime in the mid-1990s, Preston wrote me a letter and included with it a copy of a letter written to him by his long-time best friend, Johnny Otis, who'd produced a number of Top 10 pop hits in the fifties and sixties, including "Willy and the Hand Jive" and "Every Beat of My Heart," made famous by Gladys Knight and the Pips. Preston's purpose in sending me the letter was to acquaint me with the male point of view regarding adultery and philandering and to make the point that he *himself* had been quite accepting of my opinions and dissenting views, despite the fact that even his closest friend found me to be outrageously and inappropriately outspoken.

Johnny's letter detailed his disgust and disappointment in me for outing Preston in what he considered to be a mean-spirited and malicious manner. In Johnny's opinion, he and Preston had been doing what every man has a right to do—and in fact *should* be doing. Johnny's conclusion to Preston was that I was an ungrateful daughter who should be shut out and cut off—or, at the very least, straightened out, before having further access to him. He wrote that their days of chasing women outside of their marriages were the best of their lives. He and Preston called these women "Clarks," because when they spoke of them in their wives' presences, they assigned male names to them to avoid arousing suspicion.

As I read Preston's and Johnny's letters over and over again, trying to sort it all out, self-doubt and negativity pervaded my thoughts. I waffled between thinking Preston and Johnny to be arrogant, self-absorbed, and sexist men, and believing myself to be indisputably petty, whiny, self-pitying, and recalcitrant. After much internal debate, I have finally concluded that the truth lies somewhere in the middle, and that in this, as well as in all areas of my life, it is ultimately less damaging and easier to love and forgive them and myself than to stew and hate. What earthly good would it do me to spend another second of my life being angry or hurt about the things I believe I was denied? Certainly, there were many times in my childhood when any sort of financial or emotional help would have meant a world of difference to us, times when I ached to have someone other than my unstable mother looking out for us. But that simply didn't happen, and life went on anyway. Our father was not there to ease any of the tension that Lisa and I grew up with, nor was he there to provide emotional support once we met him, yet here I am, happy, healthy, and living a fine life anyway. Somehow, I believe I just grew tired of nursing my "sacred wound." For whatever reason, maybe the simple passage of time or maybe the security and comfort I now enjoy, it began to feel silly to me and self-indulgent to spend so much time mourning the deprivation of a life I never had. It occurred to me that much of the strength and self-sufficiency I've developed over the years has been directly attributable to the way I grew up. I also realized that nothing my mother or father or society had done to me had prevented me from pursuing my own happiness.

It is easy to blame Preston, but in matters of love and relationship, I've often fallen short myself. That Preston has, against all odds, stayed married to the same woman for nearly six decades and remains a strong, loving, and constant presence to Norman, Richie, Portia, and Preston Junior is an undeniably remarkable feat for anyone, much more so a black man growing up within the shadow of institutionalized slavery. I am told that Preston's mother, Mexie Love, was over 103 years old when she died in Omaha in the 1980s. This would mean that her parents, Preston's grandparents, were most likely held as slaves. Perhaps they had legally migrated from Texas to Nebraska after emancipation. Or perhaps they came north as runaways, enduring a journey undoubtedly treacherous and terrifying. I will never know. My great-grandparents' stories lay untold and unwritten, yet are recorded in my and Preston's blood and skin, our cellular memory.

MOVING ON

❦

Nineteen seventy-six proved to be a pivotal year for me. Besides leaving home with my sister and meeting my father, I also met a twenty-four-year-old guitar player named Leroy Bates, who had attended one of my father's shows. Having seen me sing with my father's band and not knowing how else to reach me, Leroy came to my high school chorus class and asked my teacher if he might speak with me. He explained that he and some other musicians who'd heard me that night had obtained a grant to perform music at the Nebraska State Penitentiary. They wondered if I wanted to audition for the position of lead singer in their band. I did and, after a few rehearsals, I was singing Chaka Khan and Aretha Franklin songs to a group of mostly black convicts on a prison stage. I made fifty dollars for that, my first paying gig, and was thrilled with the whole experience, which led to a friendship I still enjoy with Leroy.

Throughout my senior year, I continued to resent Martin for the ease his race and class afforded him. I picked on him mercilessly and blamed him for everything, but he continued to love and care for me. Even though I treated him badly, sometime before graduation he proposed to me and gave me an engagement ring, which I accepted with some misgivings.

Leroy continued to hire me sporadically for casual gigs when he needed a singer and sometime that year, despite my promises to Martin, I began to date him. I knew this would be a huge blow to Martin, and I hid it from him. One day, Martin knocked on the door to find me somewhat disheveled. I stepped into the hallway, not inviting him in. He peered over my shoulder and saw Leroy looking guiltily back at him. I had told Leroy about Martin, but had been less than candid about the depth of our relationship. Martin, on the other hand, knew next to nothing about Leroy. It was an artless and cruel way to let him know I was no longer in love with him and had decided to abandon our plans to marry. Martin shrank from the door and ran, stricken, to the parking lot, where he drove home in his mother's car. I called him often and tried to heal some of the pain I had caused, but we were never intimate again.

In addition to making plans with Leroy, I was also making plans to attend classes at the University of Nebraska, thanks to the efforts of my high school English teacher, Merrell Grant. I had done well in her class, and she praised me often for my writing and language skills. I enjoyed reading authors and poets like William Faulkner and Langston Hughes and loved writing papers about them in her class, but I never thought it possible for me to take my interest any further than that. I assumed that after graduation, all I would do was take any full-time job I could get.

One day after school, Mrs. Grant called me to her desk and asked me what plans I had for continuing my education. Hearing that I had none, she insisted that I sit down, right that minute, and make some. I had always been fond of her, and had even gone so far as to confide in her that Lisa and I were living on our own. I wanted to follow her advice, but I could not see any possible way for me to attend college. After some investigation, she found me the funds that enabled me to attend the University of Nebraska. For that, I will always be in her debt. Throughout that first year, my tuition, my books, and even part of my living expenses were paid for by the Basic Educational Opportunity Grant she secured for me. This eased my transition from high school to college immeasurably and allowed me the time I needed to study and succeed in class. By my second year, I was nineteen years old and had decided it was time to leave the apartment I shared with Lisa and find one that I could share with Leroy. Lisa, by this time, agreed with Mom's previous complaint that I was domineering and taking advantage of her. I was indeed, by insisting that she do everything my way, from how and when we would do the dishes to how and when we would pay the rent. It was time for me to move out.

Leroy, on the other hand, had been having the time of his life for the previous two or three years, living in a large communal household with four or five other young adults. He was less than enthusiastic about leaving the home he called Fat City. The place was cheap, he had his own large bedroom, and everyone got along. Reluctant to leave, he rationalized that since Fat City was only six or seven blocks from where I lived, we were almost living together anyway. I disagreed, so I kept at him and when his two other girlfriends went on their way to other guys, I caught him in a weak moment and finally won the argument.

As I prepared to move out, my mother, who by this time had quit yet another job, had positioned herself to take my place alongside Lisa. Mom, again in financial trouble and perilously close to eviction, saw my impending departure as an opportunity and she had begun to pressure Lisa about moving into the apartment. One day, before I moved out, I overheard a phone conversation in which Mom asked Lisa yet again when I would be out of the house for good. "Why don't you ask Preston for a place to crash?" I shouted into the phone while Lisa struggled to mute the receiver. That was how our mother learned that we had met our father, and I did not stick around to hear how Lisa explained it to her. Lisa, who had never been anything in her entire life but hardworking, honest, loyal, and kind, again found herself in the painfully awkward position of having to choose between me and our mother. My mother had been mortified by my breakup with Martin, who had begun to visit her often to enlist her comfort and sympathy. Mom called Lisa daily to tell her how ruthless and cunning I had become and to warn her that I would do the same sorts of things to her if she did not save her from that fate by moving in.

In early 1979, I moved to an upstairs apartment in an older house with Leroy, literally colliding with my mother in the stairway as she carried her cardboard boxes into Lisa's apartment. Mom began her stay with Lisa by kicking her out of the alcove "bedroom" she and I had shared, and moving her onto the broken-down vinyl couch in the tiny living room. Though Lisa was out of high school and working full-time at State Farm Insurance by then, Mom immediately began chastising her for not bringing home enough money to keep her comfortably in cigarettes. Rather than ration herself, she demanded that Lisa get a second job, part-time, though Lisa herself did not smoke, and in fact had begun showing early signs of asthma. With me out of the apartment, she succeeded in shutting me completely out of our family for the next few years. Lisa told me later that our mother made no attempt in the entire two years they spent together to find a job or to contribute financially in any way to their household.

RIGHT AS RAIN

❧

By the spring of 1980, Leroy had had enough of living in the Midwest and wanted to move to the better musical opportunities in Portland, Oregon. Our lives together were not the romantic bliss I had imagined. Our downstairs neighbors were loud, intrusive, and obnoxious, and I was moody, depressed, needy, and argumentative. I missed my sister, and even, in some respects, my mother. I was nearing the end of my second year at the University of Nebraska and worked part-time driving a school bus for Lincoln Public Schools, a job for which I was totally unsuited. Though I fought with Leroy, I clung desperately to him and wished fervently to create a perfect home and to be the perfect partner. I was far from this, however, and believe that his decision to move may have been partly inspired by the way things were going between us.

It was unclear to me if Leroy was including me in his plans to leave as I overheard him making calls to friends and acquaintances in Portland, looking for temporary housing. Fearing the worst, I began to make my own plans to accompany him. I dropped out of the university at the end of the school year and gave my notice at work. I had a little money saved, and I figured it was up to him to tell me outright if he didn't want me to go with him. Looking back, I suspect that Leroy just didn't have the heart to tell me that he hoped I would volunteer to stay in Lincoln and finish my studies and that he could move on with little fanfare. He, like Martin, was a gentle, kindhearted man, and probably couldn't stand the idea of watching me fall apart as he told me that I wasn't really being invited to participate in his new life.

I couldn't bear the thought of watching him go without me, so I agonized about whether to broach the subject myself, risking rejection, or to just ignore it and hope it would go away. I decided on the former, and two weeks before we were to leave I asked him how many bags he thought I'd be able to bring.

"Hmmmmm, uhhh, well, uhhhh, gee, it doesn't look real good," he replied. I knew I had to propose something, quick, that might solve the dilemma. "I only need a few clothes and some books and that's it!" I blurted.

"Yeah, well see, ummmm . . . cuz it's still gonna be tight, ya know—even if you . . ."

"Buy my own car!" I shrieked, nearly hysterical. "That's what I'll do. I'll use some of my savings and buy my own car."

"Don'tcha think you might be better off stay—" began Leroy.

"Wow, what a dope I was not to think of that sooner," I interrupted.

"I'll get up first thing in the morning and get a newspaper to look at the car listings. Whew, I'm beat. I'm going to bed—guhnight."

I flew out of the living room and into our bedroom, leaving Leroy standing mute. I dove between the sheets and pulled the covers over my head. After a few minutes, Leroy resumed packing, and I knew I had won. Now all I had to do was buy a car with the five hundred dollars I could afford to spend. The next morning I got up at daybreak, picked up a copy of the *Journal Star,* and combed the classifieds for a car within my budget. It became apparent, immediately, that the types of vehicles that were within my budget were going to be shaky at best: "'69 Impala, looks great, needs engine $450"... "'72 Toyota, runs— $550"... "'65 Dart, runs great, needs tires, clutch, radiator, fuel pump, battery—$425." I knew Martin would have the money I needed, but realized how tacky it would be to ask him to help fund my flight to Oregon with Leroy. Even if I could find a decent car for five hundred dollars, it would leave me with only six hundred dollars.

I thought of another idea. Maybe I could ask Mrs. Grant to lend me the money. I called her up that day and asked her if I could borrow two thousand dollars to buy a reliable car. I felt wrong even as the words left my lips. She was gracious, kind, and firm in her reply. "Oh Laura, you know how fond I am of you, but I can't loan you an amount like that" had been all she had to say. I was ashamed to have even called her. I concluded that I would have to find something roadworthy for the five hundred dollars that I had to spend. That Sunday, I picked up another copy of the *Journal Star* and redoubled my efforts to find that car. An ad caught my eye: "'72 Opel 1900 station wagon—looks/runs great, $500."

A grizzled old man who sounded like he'd been smoking filterless cigarettes and driving a semi for the last seventy-five years answered the phone. "WhatcanIdoyafer?" he intoned.

"Hi, I'm calling about your Opel for sale."

"It's a great little car. You want me to bring it by and show it off?"

"Yeah, that'd be great," I enthused, forgetting that Leroy had to leave for work in a few minutes.

"Gimme yer' address then."

"Oh, hey," I said as I remembered his schedule, "my boyfriend's just leaving for work and he'll be gone till early this evening. Do you suppose you could bring it by when he gets home so he can see it, too?"

"Hey, little gal, I guess I had you wrong, you sounded like the type that made all 'er own decisions. Ain't that how modern liberated women do things these days? Them dumb guys usually get in the way's what I always thought." Offended by this insinuation that I played the obedient underling to my man, I decided to reverse course and keep our original appointment.

Twenty minutes later a bright red station wagon pulled up, bearing a man who looked exactly like he sounded. I bounded downstairs and onto the curb and extended my hand to him through the car window before he even had a chance to turn off the motor. "Hi, I'm Laura," I beamed to the sixty-something man with long dirty fingernails and a greasy pompadour haircut.

"Howdyado," he said, without removing the cigarette from his lips.

"You didn't tell me it was *red*," I gushed, already knowing I had to have this car.

The car began to sputter somewhat as it idled beside us. "I gotta 'djust the carburetor an' get it runnin' a little smoother, but it's a good little puddle jumper," he said fondly as he patted the car's hood. A persistent knocking developed as black smoke escaped from the exhaust pipe. "Yeah, that's just the way these little foreign jobs are—kinda cranky, but reliable as hell," the man said as the ash dislodged itself from the rest of the cigarette and fell to the front of his oil-soaked coveralls. "You wanna take her for a spin?" he asked, trying to speak over the banging and just as a loud rattle followed by an explosion shot from the tailpipe. The little car seemed to groan as it exhaled the last of its black smoke before dying. "Huh, she's a feisty little gal, ain't she?" the owner chuckled nervously as I began to have serious misgivings about the car. "I can get 'er started right back up though—no problem. She's right as rain," assured the man.

"Maybe I ought to let you work on it a little while and bring it back tomorrow," I offered, looking for an exit.

"Oh, there's nuthin' wrong with 'er—she's just a little cold, honey," he shot back.

"Well, okay," I surrendered, as I got into the driver's seat. Just as I reached to turn the keys in the ignition, I noticed the knob protruding from the floor between us. "Oh . . . um, gee," I began, embarrassed. "I guess I don't really know how to drive a stick shift," I admitted.

The man's eyebrows, which looked like two caterpillars, shot up as he tried to hide his surprise. A look resembling confidence replaced surprise as he began his reply. "Just let ol' Jack drive 'er for you and show you what she can do." Jack sat hunched over the steering wheel, pumping the accelerator as he tried the ignition. He tried to turn it over three or four times, to no avail, then glanced at me and smiled as he said, "I flooded 'er. She just needs a second to get 'er breath."

"Well, maybe we should just give—" I started to say just as Jack was able to gain ignition on his fifth try.

"I told ya', she's right as rain. She's purrin' like a kitten now," he assured me. As we pulled away from the curb I began to regain some of my initial enthusiasm. We had gone only about a quarter mile before Jack turned the Opel around and headed back to my apartment.

"You'd be makin' a mistake if you tried to find a better car for the money," Jack opined. "I tell ya' what. I like ladies, especially the pretty ones, so I'm gonna let 'er go for $475 to you." I still had my doubts about the car's abilities, and must have hesitated slightly before Jack exclaimed, "Ya' know, yer so pretty, I believe I'm gonna have to let you steal 'er away from me for $450."

Wow, $450, I thought. That'll give me fifty bucks more for gas and expenses on the way up there. "Okay, I'll take it," I offered, excited to be owning my own car. Jack produced the car's title from a filthy pocket and placed it on the hood of the car. "You just give me the cash and sign here where it says 'buyer' and then you take it down to the License department and get it put in your name," he instructed.

"How come there's another guy's name here where it says, 'seller'?" I asked, puzzled.

"Oh that's the guy I bought it from," Jack explained.

"Yeah, but the date here is only a week ago," I persisted.

"Uh-huh," he replied, extending his hand for the cash, offering no more information.

Maintaining my hold on my money, and still confused, I ventured, "You mean, you've only had this car one week?"

"That's right, darlin', look," said Jack, slightly impatient, "I've gotta git goin', so can we wrap this deal up?"

"Yeah, I guess so," I said, slowly placing the bills in his hand. I pulled a fifty from the wad and kept it for myself.

Jack's friendly demeanor returned as he counted and then pocketed the cash. "Yeah, that's somethin' a lotta guys do 'round here. See, you can only buy and sell seven cars a year in Nebraska before they consider you a dealer. Then o'course ya gotta get a dealer's license, and that'll set you back *thousands*. So, I just buy 'em, work on 'em, and turn 'em over before the date expires when you gotta have 'em registered in your name, and the state don't even know."

"So, you sorta do this for a living?" I asked.

"Uh-huh," he answered.

"Do you make an okay living doing that?" I continued.

"Yeah, pretty good," he answered. "I buy most of 'em dead for next to nothin'. I got an acre just outside of town. I prob'ly got sixty junkers sittin' there. Once I get 'em goin', I unload 'em."

"I see. So, are you like a mechanic or something?"

"Nope, I just kinda always enjoyed tinkerin' around with cars. This one's the first Opel I've ever had, though. They're kinda rare in the States—hard to get parts for, one of a kind. Hey, I gotta walk up to the corner and hop a bus downtown. Good luck with it." And with that Jack headed south toward A Street and out of my life.

Buyer's remorse set in immediately as I looked over the rare, one-of-a-kind vehicle I'd just purchased. Leroy came home that evening and looked shocked as I showed off my latest acquisition. "You bought an Opel!" he gasped, incredulous. "You'll never be able to get parts for that thing," he moaned.

"Well, why would I need parts?" I countered. "Jack said this thing is 'reliable as hell.'"

"Well, I'm sure he got the 'hell' part right," quipped Leroy, to my irritation. He poked his head into the driver's side window and read the odometer. "Jesus Christ, this thing's got damn near two hundred thousand miles on it," he lamented.

"See, I told you it was reliable," I sneered back.

"That's not good news, Jonesy," he said quietly, placing his arm around my shoulder. I dismissed his doubt-filled stare and asked him for a quick lesson in operating a manual transmission, hoping to distract him from voicing any more of his concerns.

Leroy slid behind the steering wheel as I handed him the keys. He leaned an ear toward the dash before turning the key. He seemed to believe he could tell, just by the sound of the motor firing up, the exact roadworthiness and condition of the car. I held my breath as he turned the key. It might have been comical had this been someone else's car is-suing such a high-pitched stutter and pouring black smoke into the air, but I found no humor in my predicament. Leroy turned off the ignition and waited a second as I explained to him that it was "just flooded." After a number of attempts, he started the car and left it running while he checked under the hood. Of course, that's what you do, I thought, you look under the hood. Leroy's face began to take on a tragic pallor as he examined the dipstick. "Hmmm, this doesn't look good," he muttered.

"What's that?" I asked, dejected.

"Well, there's a lot of water in the oil, and that's not a good sign."

"How come?" I asked, not really wanting to know.

"It could mean any number of bad things," he answered, sadly.

"Look, Leroy, all it has to do is get me to Portland. We'll car cara-van. It'll be all right. It's a station wagon so all my stuff will fit into it. Let's just give it a chance," I pleaded.

"Yeah, okay," Leroy said, reluctantly.

NORTHWEST
PASSAGE

❧

Two weeks *later Leroy* and I left our apartment for the last time. The Opel was running a little better by then, thanks to the donated labor of Leroy and his friends. It had trouble climbing hills, but I had faith it would get me to Portland. Leroy and I had decided to maintain the speed limit for the entire distance and to always be within each other's sight should anything go wrong. We pulled away from our curb and off we went. My heart crawled into my throat as I entered the westbound I-80 on-ramp. I kept my eyes on Leroy's '71 Dart and tried not to cry as I put my car into high gear and settled in for the long drive ahead. Five minutes in, I looked up into my rearview mirror and noticed the perfect frame it provided for the capitol. There was no going

back now. Seeing the glint of that golden dome reaching into the perfect blue sky as I drove across the wide open prairie pushed me over the
edge. I embraced the steering wheel as if it were my mother, locking
my arms gently behind it as I pulled myself closer and cried.

We stayed on I-80 as we reached Grand Island, Kearney, North Platte,
Ogallala, and then Sidney. Though I'd lived in Nebraska all of my life, I
had rarely ventured outside Lincoln, and my senses were bathed in the
sights and sounds of the prairie. Pheasants, meadowlarks, cardinals,
and sandhill cranes met my eyes as I scanned the wheatfields and corn-
fields. Cattails sprang up right beside the road wherever marshes survived the surrounding development. Hawks, hoping to spy preoccupied
prairie dogs, perched on the telephone poles that lined the freeway. I
often found myself trying to imagine the plains before European set-
tlers had arrived.

A couple of days and hundreds of miles into our trip, I noticed that
we were nearing the area where Mount Saint Helens had blown her
top a couple of months earlier. I'd heard it was still quite active and
that intrigued me. I had been excited the previous spring to hear that a
natural disaster of this magnitude had taken place so close to where
Leroy had been threatening to move. At that point, I'd hoped the event
would put the kibosh on the move, but instead it sparked further interest. Driving along, we both noticed the thickening air. Leroy thrust his
hand, palm up, out of his window, indicating his own desire for rain.
The haze continued to thicken until the sun all but disappeared behind
it. We both realized that we were driving through the ash that still lin-
gered in the air from the volcano. We knew the mountain had blown a
few times since the big one, but actually driving through the fallout
was an experience I'll never forget.

About ten miles past La Grande, with two hundred miles to go before we reached Portland, I glanced down at my dashboard. I had continued to lose power that day and could barely reach fifty miles per hour on a flat surface. Now, it seemed, I was about to become a bottle rocket. I had not seen Leroy in the last fifteen or twenty minutes and struggled with the idea of pulling off the road and letting the car cool off, versus trying to catch up with him as my car became engulfed in flames. I pushed on, but before long, steam billowed out from under my hood.

There was little traffic in sight as I pulled the car into the emergency lane and sat there wondering what to do. Half an hour passed as I sat there in that inferno fretting about the Opel and wishing Leroy would appear. Just as I got up to stretch my legs, Leroy did appear. He cooled down the engine, and miraculously it started, but not without a fight. It rattled and pinged and knocked and finally coughed a mighty spasm as it shuddered to life. Smoke flumed out the back end as I looked anxiously at Leroy. "What do you think?" I asked, cautiously.

"Well, we don't have money to tow it anywhere, so let's go," he advised.

I put it into gear and we eased the ten miles into Pendleton, where we found a service station.

A middle-aged mechanic checked out the car but his prognosis was grim. Even if the parts for the car had been available, it would take days and a lot of money to fix it. Leroy offered to mash whatever clothes would fit into his already overstuffed Dart, and to drive us both on to Portland. Miserable, I agreed. Sometime around midnight, we hauled our exhausted bodies up to Leroy's friend Dana's unlocked door. We fell in a heap onto the foam mattress he had laid in his basement office and slept like the dead until well into the next morning.

After a hearty breakfast, Dana offered to give us a tour of the city. He loaded us into his VW van and drove us into the city. I discovered that Dana's house was located in the southeast section of town, which he advised might be a little more than we could afford. He recommended the Northwest Industrial area as a suitable place to hunt for inexpensive housing. He pulled onto a street called Burnside and headed west toward a bridge, which he said would be coming right up. A musty odor pervaded the air as we drove and I asked him what it was. "Those are pulp mills," he explained. "They stink, don't they?"

"I'll say," I agreed. We pulled onto the Burnside Bridge as I gazed into the muddy water below.

"That's the Willamette River," he said, with the emphasis on the "am." "Portland's a pretty mellow place, and I think you'll like it. I'm going to give you a little tip that's going to make life a lot easier for you here. I don't want you guys to have to learn this the hard way like I did, so I'm going to set you up. There are only two things you can do to really fuck up around here," Dana said, gravely, as he stopped at an intersection overlooking the magnificent Fremont Bridge. He turned to face me and looked directly into my eyes as I sat, rapt, in the passenger seat next to him. "If you can avoid making these two mistakes, you're going to have it made," he continued. By this time Leroy was on the edge of his seat, too. Dana leaned in close and pointed his finger at us for emphasis. "Never call that river we just crossed 'the *William*-ette,' and never call this state we're in 'Ore-*gone*.'" That piece of advice has stayed with me the entire twenty-odd years I have lived in the Pacific Northwest.

EPILOGUE

Moving to Portland with Leroy marked the beginning of what I now think of as the second phase of my life. It also began a nearly two-year absence from my sister's life, as well as what was to become a sixteen-year loss of communication with my mother. Many years have passed and now, in my forties, I live in Seattle, Washington, making my living as a musician, singer, and songwriter. In 1987, I resumed my studies at the University of Washington and graduated with honors in the field of psychology. I've made peace with the past and come to see each event as a gift from which I have received strength, kindness, and understanding. Over the years my need to control others and to be angry has abated. Instead I work to find common ground and acceptance.

My mother and father gave me a lot: love and ability for music as well as the strength and determination to succeed in this difficult business. I understand now that my mother did the best she could with what she had. I spent all of my childhood and a good deal of my adulthood judging her by the same standards I would a mentally healthy individual. Seeing her as cruel or sadistic did little to serve either of us. As recently as a few years ago, it was confusing to me that someone so intelligent and capable in so many ways could not cope with life's most basic challenges and provide the loving, stable, nurturing home Lisa and I yearned for. It is clear to me now that she was not born with the tools she needed to be whole.

I think about both my mother and my father nearly every day. It is difficult for me, as I look around and see all that I have achieved, to feel damaged by my upbringing. I think back often to the time we spent living in the Lincoln City Mission, or Cedar's, or visiting my mother at the Nebraska State Hospital and wonder at the extraordinary reliance my family has had on government-sponsored programs and publicly funded institutions. What might have become of us had there been no safety nets such as Aid to Dependent Children, food stamps, free medical clinics, and Head Start, of which I was one of the first graduates? Without emergency housing for families, we would have otherwise been homeless.

As bad as things often got, I can look around me now, living in the city of Seattle, and see how much worse it could have been. I volunteered in a downtown homeless shelter years ago, where we often had to turn people away because of our limited space and resources, and we were in constant jeopardy of losing what little funding we had. I found it excruciating to have to close the doors to young mothers in crisis, simply because every bed and cot was occupied. If there had been no Planned Parenthood, where throughout my teenage years I was able to get free birth control and counseling, would I have become a young, homeless single mother? President Jimmy Carter's Basic Educational Opportunity Grant provided a way for me to start college, and with the encouragement of Mrs. Grant, I became a 4.0 student that first year at the University of Nebraska. Had it not been for government-funded scholarship programs and watchful, caring teachers like Kathy French and Merrell Grant, my outcome might have been quite different.

Looking back, particularly on those first months living on my own, I can see how precariously I walked between choosing a life dominated by lying and stealing and operating outside of society—a life ruled by bitterness and a sense of disenfranchisement—and that of wanting to be part of a just community and all it has to offer. I realize how astute my mother was when she explained what Shakespeare meant when he wrote, "The quality of mercy is not strained," and encouraged us to try to live our lives with that in mind. At many critical points along the way, someone or something positive threw itself in my path, tipping the scales from despair to hope, from pain to promise.

These experiences have led me, politically, all the way to the left of center. I have seen firsthand how vital social welfare programs are to the stability of our communities, and I am baffled by the constant barrage of attacks by unsympathetic politicians to their existence. I know that these safety nets work and I wonder each day why we are not doing more to bolster and expand them and to create new programs. Having had so little growing up, I am easily delighted by small comforts and am content with all the gifts my career has afforded me.

Through my music, I have been able to travel the world and experience the profoundly beautiful and wild places we still have left in this country. This travel has shaped my world view to include a deep and abiding belief that we must do everything within our power to strengthen and enhance environmental protection, that we may all, someday, be able to see what I have seen, and more. I would never have guessed, growing up so preoccupied with my own troubles, that there was a natural world outside of Lincoln, so magnificent and fragile.

In the fall of 2002 I became a foster mother to a seven-month-old blond, blue-eyed baby girl who came to me from far less than ideal circumstances. I, who never imagined myself to be a mother to anything but homeless cats, now fill my days changing diapers and reading books like *Princess Smartypants*. I have the love of a child who was removed from her birth home with eight broken bones. My partner, Pam, and my best friend, Mary, and I have watched her magical transformation from an apprehensive, eerily quiet baby to a laughing, screaming, cooing, gurgling, squirming mass of perpetual motion. She seems to be bursting outward with joy and life. Our household has been turned upside down by the truckload of toys and musical instruments that litter our living room floor. When we crank up the hi-fi, she bounces and squeals, turns in circles and claps, especially for the recordings of Tim and Mollie O'Brien. In the evening, when the cats surround me and the baby has fallen asleep and lies peacefully in her crib, I reflect on the goodness of life.

Through my experiences, I have learned, perhaps above all else, that we humans are truly defined more by our similarities than our differences. We are equally entitled to the beauty and bounty of this delicate place, and we are all equally obligated to care for it and for each other.

Against all odds, it would seem, my mother, father, and his wife, Betty, are still living. Preston just celebrated his eightieth birthday and still gigs in Omaha. What a fine thing that his children, Norman, Richie,

Portia, and Preston Junior, were able to experience the security of having both a devoted father and loving mother present in their home as they grew up. I have recently begun a phone relationship with Portia that allows me to laugh and wonder at the goodness of having family surface in unexpected places and times.

Lisa and I have again become close and consider ourselves to be ridiculously lucky and blessed to have survived it all with so much. At times we bring each other to tears laughing uncontrollably about some terrifying event in our past that once gave us great pain. I no longer store rage that I didn't have a "normal" upbringing, that life was hard, that my father was absent, that my mother was crazy and unpredictable. I no longer relive moments of shame caused by poverty, mental illness, racism, sexism, and classism. The insults to me, my mother, and my sister, although horrific at times and seemingly endless, each had a function in shaping who I have become. Each day I am surrounded by music and laughter and filled with love. As the days pass I am visited evermore with gentle thoughts and empathy for those who may not have been kind to me when I wanted them to be. As I think about how my life has gone, I am increasingly convinced that in all those sad years, the only obstacle to my own happiness was the mistaken notion that I had been deprived. Today, my challenge is to remember how perfect life really is, rather than to regret what was, and to remind myself often how glorious and sweet it is to be, and to remain . . . satisfied.